AF556336

GROWTH OF FISHNET INDUSTRY

GROWTH OF FISHNET INDUSTRY

By

Dr. D. Andrews Scott
Assistant Professor
Dept. of Commerce
Alagappa Govt Arts College, Karaikudi
Tamil Nadu
(India)

&

Dr. R. Pon Murugan
Senior Researcher
Dept. of Commerce
Madurai Kamaraj University, Madurai
Tamil Nadu
(India)

DISCOVERY PUBLISHING HOUSE PVT. LTD.
NEW DELHI-110 002

Published by:
Tilak Wasan

DISCOVERY PUBLISHING HOUSE PVT. LTD.
4383/4B, Ansari Road, Darya Ganj
New Delhi-110 002 (India)
Phone : +91-11-23279245, 43596064-65
Fax : +91-11-23253475
E-mail : parul.wasan@gmail.com
discoverypublishinghouse@gmail.com
web : www.discoverypublishinggroup.com

***First Edition:* 2012**

ISBN: 978-93-5056-089-1

Growth of Fishnet Industry

Printed at:
Shree Balaji Art Press
Delhi

Preface

Modernisation through research and development has become inevitable in every segment of modern of life. To cope with the modern development, especially after globlisation, every industrial segment has been preparing themselves for a transformation. In the process of regeneration every industrial process is equipped with modern devices and gadgets. As an outcome the industrial production has merely doubled with more precision without any deterioration in quality.

Fishing being the pertinent industrial segment generating not merely the essential feed needed for the daily livelihood of even the poor, but the foreign exchange to the exchequer modernised its crafts and gears. Since harvesting of fish mainly depends upon the nets used for catching, the units manufacturing fishnets in the country had a good opportunity some years ago. But the globalisation brought many new foreign marketers to the country and the market of the day becomes a challenging and competitive one especially to Indian small scale manufacturers.

By the time the scarce labour market due to poor salary structure aggravated the problem to the local manufacturers. In this scenario the author probed the industry from dawn to dusk in Kanyakumari the southern most district in Indian continent, where the industry blossoms. The analysis substantiated with statistical evidences and tests really kindles the eagerness of the reader to know more on the issue.

The problems focussed touches the minds of the entrepreneurs who are engaged in the field. The most appropriate suggestion forwarded in the study consoles them with the expectation that the day for solving their problem is not far away from them.

In their maiden effort the authors have achieved their mission through the message what they profounded in the book. It is earnestly hoped that since it addresses the issues in fishnets industry in the right direction, it will reach the concerned authorities and show a green signal of prosperity to the industry. Further the humble work has brought to light all issues without neglecting anything in the industry. Hence this could well educate many of the younger educationalists and budding researchers on the field.

Dr. D. Andrews Scott
Dr. R. Pon Murugan

Contents

Introduction and Design of the Study

INTRODUCTION

Two-thirds of the global area is covered by sea water. The sea is not only the store house of water but also a store of resources like food and valuable commodities such as pearl[1] medicines and raw materials for industries. The sea is a good supplier of food in the form of fish. Fish has become an important part of diet for millions of people throughout the world especially in the coastal regions. It is estimated that human population is presently increasing at approximately 2 per cent a year and 10 to 30 million people die due to starvation or deceased by malnutrition. Fish could be a mitigating force in supplying food to the world. At present more than 90 million tonnes of fish are harvested from world seas annually. Fishing is one of the most familiar economic activities associated with the sea. 'Fishing' refers to the landing of all types of marine and fresh water 'Faunas'[2].

India is one of the important fishing nations of the world[3]. India is a developing country which stands second in population next to China. People in India mainly depend on agriculture for their livelihood. Next to agriculture fishing plays a prominent role in the country. India has a coastal line of 8,129 km. The 7.5 million hectares of fresh water bodies and 1.4 million brackish water bodies such as estuarine, backwater and mangrove water ways existing in the country meet the fishing requirements of the country. India's annual fish production is 4.95 million tones (2.825 million tons from the sea and 2.125 million tons from inland water bodies) during 2005-2006 and the share of aquaculture is nearly 0.144 million tons.

India is the third largest fish producer in the world with a total production of 4.2 million tonns for the year 2003-2004. The harvestable potential of marine fishery resources in the EEZ (Exclusive Economic Zone) has been estimated at about 3.921 million tons[4]. The fishing resources in the country are distributed as: inshore (58 per cent) offshore (34.9%) and deep sea (7%). Growth of fish production has been about 4.12 per cent per annum during the 1990's. However, the full potential of fishing has not been realised[5].

In India, Tamil Nadu is one of the important maritime states with rich inland and marine resources. It has a coastline of 1076 km and accounts for 15 per cent of the total fish landing in India. Roughly one-fourth of all marine exports from the country is from Tamil Nadu. According to a census taken by the Fisheries Department of the Government of Tamil Nadu, there are 556 marine fishing villages in Tamil Nadu, which has a population of about 6.70 lakhs, out of which 2.62 lakhs fisherman are actively engaged in fishing. At present 53,684 mechanised boats, 44,578 motorised traditional craft and 1,81,284 non-motorised traditional crafts are engaged in fishing[6].

In Tamil Nadu, Kanyakumari is a major district engaging actively in fishing. Marine fishing is one of the major industries of Kanyakumari district. The coastal eco-system of this district comprises 68 km in length and is studded with 44 fishing villages. Its contribution for socio-economic upliftment of the coastal population in the district is noteworthy. The total fishermen population of Kanyakumari district is 1,33,264 (24.77% of the total fishermen population of the state) of which 48,306 (36.25%) fishermen were engaged in fishing[7]. The Kanyakumari district has a total population of 16,76,034 in 2001[8].

TECHNOLOGICAL TRANSFORMATIONS

Modern fishing is evolved through three main technological revolutions. The first revolution is mechanisation of fishing crafts which began in late 19th century with the use of steam propulsion fishing vessels which was followed by steam driven winches. The second revolution in modern fishing is the use of eco-sounding and eco-ranging equipments and navigators in fishing vessels. (Navigator is a satellite programmed equipment, which shows or identifies the directions where the last catch was made). The third major revolution in modern fishing is the advent of synthetic fibres, such as nylon which totally revolutionised the fishing industry.

Prior to 1950's fishing nets were made of natural materials like cotton, flax and sisal. These nets tended to knot and break easily after usage. Further, these nets absorbed water and made the fishing hard. A variety of sizes of yarns were used in the traditional nets. These nets could not be repaired because of the use of poor quality yarn. However, with the advent of synthetic materials, stronger, long lasting light weight nets were manufactured. This made the fishing industry to work efficiently. Synthetic fibres used for modern fishing are of high quality. There are several varieties of fishnets manufactured using synthetic fibres.

The synthetic fibres are made up of nylon, polyethylene, vinylon, polyester and polypropylene. Using these fibres, high quality nets are made. For different applications different types of nets made up of either monofilament (single filament is used) or multifilament (more than one filament is used) are used. Each filament (either mono or multi filament) has different strength which depends upon the thickness and weight of the filament.

In order to make a multifilament, the basic yarn (single fiber filament) is converted in to a twine (multifilament) using machines. In net making, several of such mono or multifilament twines are knitted together by knots. Knitting of nets is carried out through two types of knots. They are single and double knots. In a single knot net, either two or more mono or multifilament yarns are joined together with a single knot. But in case of double knot net, two or more mono filament or multifilament twines are joined together with double knots. The basic difference between these types of knots is that double knot nets are much stronger than the single knot nets. Double knots are resistant to damages by rough and tough usage. Hence, in trawling double knot multifilament nets are used.

MODERNISATION OF FISHING GEARS

When the technology got improved, the hand made nets started to lose their importance. In their place machines were introduced. The net manufacturing machines produced nets with greater consistency in quality and higher strength than the nets manufactured by manual labour. The volume of production of nets has also considerably increased. During 1980's, Japan was the leading fishing net manufacturer and was exporting to various countries all over the world. Because of the increased wages and higher manufacturing cost in Japan, manufacturing of fishnet was found uneconomical. During this time Korea and Taiwan entered in the field and dominated the world market. During 1985, both Korea and Taiwan also faced the problem of increased manufacturing costs. Hence, production and export from those countries gradually started declining. By this time, the scope for production of fishing nets in developing countries including India brightened in view of low wages and power charges[9]. Using this opportunity, many small scale and large scale units started their operations in India and the existing units started to increase their capacity. Since then the fishnet units in India have been increasing in number.

STATEMENT OF THE PROBLEM

Unemployment, poverty, food scarcity, nutritional deficiency, inadequate foreign exchange and the like are the main challenges to the Indian economy. Fisheries play an important role in providing full-time and part-time employment to a group of people (who are unemployed). It is reported that 1466 million people got employment in the sector in India in 2003-2004[10]. Further the food it supplies to the society is very much nutritious than any other food. It is also a major contributor to foreign exchange and the contribution of this sector to the country's GDP is remarkable. Fisheries sector contributed 1.07 per cent to the GDP of the country in 2003-2004. The foreign exchange generated by the sector was U.S. $ 1365 million during the year 2004[11]. The demand for fish is increasing year by year along with the increasing population. It is estimated that India would need 94,28,000 to 1,26,11,000 tones of fish by year 2030. In other words the growth in domestic demand for fish would range between 121 per cent and 195 per cent[12]. Thus, India needs to pay a special attention to its fishing Industry.

Most of the fisher-folk in India are very poor and illiterate and fishing is carried out in a primitive manner using small frail boats, catamarans and vallams. Fighting against the wind and the tide is a major problem to the traditional crafts in fishing. The traditional crafts were not able to go beyond a narrow distance about 4 to 7 km into the sea. It is estimated that the traditional fishermen were able to tap only 10 per cent of the entire fishable marine area. So naturally mechanisation of the crafts and modernisation of the gears seem to be the solution for this problem[13]. The growth of fishing industry depends on the mechanisation of fishing crafts, modernisation of fishing gears and development of fishing infrastructure. In mechanisation of fishing craft, the traditional catamaran and vallam have become outdated and boats with outboard engines and inbuilt engines are used in fishing. In the development of fishing infrastructure, fishing harbours have been constructed in the major fishing centers. But mechanisation of crafts and development of infrastructure will be futile if modernisation of gear is not attempted. Modernisation of fishing gears call for the use of synthetic fibre in fishing nets. Accordingly, fishnet manufacturing has become an interlinked and supplementary industry to the fishing industry. Beyond contributing to the fishing industry, the fishnet industry earns its significance for its employment opportunities, promotion of entrepreneurship, regional economic development, contribution to GDP and foreign exchange revenue.

Fishnet industry in India has its recent origin. However, the growth recorded in the recent past is greater than the growth recorded in the past 30 years. The same is the trend in Kanyakumari district. Fishnet manufacturing has become one of the major industries in Kanyakumari district. The growth of fishnet industry in the district has not only provided employment opportunities but also contributed to the economic development. The mushrooming growth of fishnet manufacturing units in the district has led to competition among fishnet units. The stiff competition existing among the units to capture the market has considerably reduced the profitability.

Interrupted production due to shortage of labour and seasonal demand for fishnet has led to under utilisation of capacity which is a signal of sickness in the industry. This has lead to closure of many units. The closure of fishnet units has made many employees unemployed and the industrial production of the district has come down. The fishnet requirements of the fishing folk are not met. This has affected fish production. The instability in fishnet industry in Kanyakumari district has stagnated the industrial development of the district. The stagnation in fishnet industry has led to a major threat with respect to industrial development in Kanyakumari district. It raises the following issues:

(i) To what extent have fishnet units grown in Kanyakumari district?

(ii) If not, what have been the factors which limit their growth in Kanyakumari district?

There are no studies so for attempted to find answers to the above questions. Hence, a serious attempt to probe the above issues is needed. This empirical study is planned on the above dimensions to fill such a gap.

REVIEW OF PREVIOUS STUDIES

The review of literature of the past research studies on the subject is attempted in this part. There is very limited literature available on the subject. However, a few important studies related to fishing gears have been reviewed here. Such a review facilitated the researcher to have a comprehensive knowledge on the subject, which enabled the researcher to adopt, modify and formulate an improved conceptual frame work for the present study.

Kurien and Mathew (1978) in the study titled, "Impact of technological changes in fishing among fishermen" identified that there are wide regional variations in the species-mix of the marine resources in the country. The nutritive value of all species of fish is almost the same. There is a direct impact of mechanisation of fish production in quantitative as well a qualitative nature[14].

Day (1979) studied the need for fisheries development in Sri Lanka, India, Bangladesh, Pakistan and South Yemen. Improvement in handling, distribution and marketing of fish, strengthening and extension services were found to be the urgent needs of fishermen for their socio-economic improvement[15].

Bhushan, (1979) studied the impact of mechanisation of fishing craft on small fishermen. He revealed the fact that the small fishermen have not been able to reap the benefits of mechanisation[16].

Tendel (1981) studied the 'Operational constraints of fishermen along the Karnataka coast'. The use of purse seine and trawl nets were reported to have caused serious damages to the economy of fishermen, particularly those depending on shore based operations for their livelihood. The study concluded that improvement in the traditional gears would help the fishermen to overcome the operational difficulties[17].

Sreenivasan (1981) worked on "Economics of various types of fishing crafts operated in Tamil Nadu". The return per unit investment of non-powered boats was estimated to be twice that of powered boats. The traditional fishing crafts generated almost seven times the direct employment provided by the mechanised boat categories. It was suggested that the additional income and employment could be generated through fishnets manufacturing, fish processing and fish marketing[18].

Kurien (1981) analysed the causes for the poverty among the fishermen. According to his report, inequality in the asset holdings among fisherman, exploitation by market intermediaries and the habit of excessive spending during high catch season are the three main reasons for poverty among the fishing households[19].

Advani, (1981) in the study "Small scale sector cracking up", analysed the growth of the small scale industries during the period 1972-79 with reference to the growth in the number of units, fixed capital, employment, output and the total value added. The study covered all the state and union territories in India. Based on his micro-analysis he concluded that for the economy as a whole, the figures were highly impressive[20].

Sathiyadhas (1982) conducted the study titled "Mechanisation of indigenous crafts with out-board motors in Tamil Nadu" which examined the impact of mechanisation of indigenous crafts with outboard motors in Tamil Nadu. The major finding of the study is that there is not much difference between the total catche volume of motorised and non-motorised catamaran in Tirunelveli district. Due to motorisation, employment opportunity was doubled since the motorised catamaran required three to five persons instead of only two for the non-motorised units[21].

Khakhar and Patel (1984) have examined the impact technological changes on the fishermen community of Sourashtra region. They studied the economic, social and cultural determinants of technological changes and related aspects[22].

Sathiadhas and Panikar (1985) analysed the cost and earning of trawlers of different sizes, namely 8.5m, 9.0 m and 10.0 m operating at the Tuticorin harbour during 1985. The economic parameters like annual fixed cost, operation cost, gross revenue and net profit were studied. The indicators of economic efficiency like the rate of return on capital, capital-turnover ratio and cost of production per kilogram of fish production were estimated[23].

Srivastava and Dharma Reddy (1986) the studied the impact of mechanisation on small fishermen. This study is unique in the sense that for the first time the impact of mechanisation was studied in depth. The study provides insights into the problems of small fishermen in the midst of technological changes[24].

Bindhyachal et al. (1987) analysed the economics of the fish landings of mechanised and non-mechanised crafts in Vizakapatinam of the Andhra coast. The samples of mechanised and traditional units were studied to estimate fish production. The returns were estimated by taking into consideration the fixed and variable costs. The mechanised crafts were found to provide more employment opportunities for more fishermen[25].

Selvaraj (1988) studied "The economics of different craft categories in selected coastal fishing villages of Kanyakumari district of Tamil Nadu" and identified the fishing seasons for important species of fish groups. He formulated strategies for the development of the fisheries sector and for the betterment of the fisher folk in the district.

Senthilathiban and Selvaraj (1988) carried out "the financial statement analysis for different fishing crafts operated in the fishing villages of Tirunelveli district". The highest solvency ratio was worked out for mechanised boats and the lowest for vallam with out-board engine. The positive net worth for all the craft categories showed that their occupation was sound and that the business was in an adequately solvent condition.

Mathiarjunan (1989) assessed "the annual fishing cost and returns of the various types of fishing crafts in Tuticorin coast" and estimated the influence of the important dependent variables of fish production. His study also analysed some of the efficiency measures like the rate of return in capital, cost of fish production per kilogram, and input output ratio. A fishery production function was also estimated to assess the impact of explanatory variables namely boat length, horse power, fuel, gear length, fuel cost and the age of fishermen on the value of fish catch. The co-efficient of horse power, fuel cost and age of fishermen were all found to be positive and significant[26].

Annamalai and Kandoran (1990) studied the economics of motorised traditional crafts. The cost of fitting an outboard motor was as substantial as the cost of acquiring a new fishing craft. Besides, there arose the requirement of few more types of low cost gear after motorisation. The cost and return data for the motorised traditional crafts were analysed and the fishing trips were reported with inadequate gross returns even to meet the fuel coat. The introduction of engine had necessitated the requirement of fuel for every trips and the survival of fishing units was found to depend on the financial capacity of fishermen[27].

Pazhani (1998) the study to highlight the financial status of fishermen households. They did so by analyzing the source of credit, repayment, assets and liabilities also the credit utilisation behaviour of fishermen. Further, they also workedout the outstanding debt per household in the catamaran and motorised catamaran sectors. The study, thus, brought out the reason for the poor repayment of loans[28].

Eggert (2001) examined the level of technical efficiency for a sample of Swedish trawlers which mainly targeted Norway lobster, Shrimp and demersal fish. The data on per-trip gross revenues, fishing effort, gear choice, month of fishing and vessel attribute are analysed using a translog stochastic production frontier, including a model for vessel-specific technical inefficiencies. The inefficiency model indicates that efficiency decreases with total annual effort and the same applies with vessel size. Further, it is found that older vessels are less efficient[29].

Fency, S.A. (2001) in her study titled "A descriptive study of fishnet industry in Kanyakumari District" has analysed the structure of the industry in Kanyakumari district and the reasons for its concentration in the district, its employment potential and the various problems faced by it. She concludes that the industry is profitable with a thin margin rate and giving substantial employment opportunity to women. She suggests for diversification of products, provision of welfare facilities to workers and effective intervention of Fishnet Industry Association in the development of the industry[30].

Pascoe and Colglan (2002), in their study on the contribution of immeasurable inputs to fishery production analysed the efficiency of trawlers. The most important factor affecting efficiencies was the age of vessel. However, immeasurable factors accounted for more than about 65 per cent of the variation in efficiency, and as much as 9 per cent of the total variation in catches between boats[31].

Sathasivalingom (2002) in his study titled "A study on fishnet industries in Kanyakumari district" attempted to analyse the growth of fishnet units in Kanyakumari district in terms of production and marketing of fishnet. He has also analysed the marketing mechanism adopted in this industry. His study also highlights the various deficiencies of the entrepreneurs which affect its profitability[32].

Antony Raj (2002) in his study on "Export trade of marine products in India" probed, how the modern gears were used by craft owners. The fishing gears are used in different crafts at different seasons. The traditional crafts using fishermen normally use hook and lines, sardine net, shrimp net and ray nets. The motorised craft use gillnets, azila nets and tuna nets in addition to the above hooks and lines and sardine net. But mechanised craft uses generally trawl nets and gillnet and some times hooks and lines[33].

Kramer (2003) in his study on "Artisnal Fisheries in Malaysia" revealed the fact that artisanal fishers are poor, but enjoy a higher level of technical efficiency. It suggests that targeted development assistance to the harvesting sector may be better directed to other priorities in artisanal fishing communities[34].

SCOPE OF THE STUDY

The present study is an attempt to analyse the growth of fishnet units in Kanyakumari district. Growth of fishnet units can be studied from the angle of the owners who own the fishnet units. Similarly, the same could also be gauged from the stand point of the government which controls the industry. In this study, the growth of fishnet units has been looked from the angle of the entrepreneurs who run the unit.

The study focuses on the variables measuring the growth of fishnet industry. In the course of analysis, the relationship between growth and entrepreneurship is also studied. At the end part of the study the factors that are contributing towards the growth in fishnet industry are analysed.

OBJECTIVES OF THE STUDY

The following are the specific objectives of the study:

(i) To study the growth of fishnet industry in Kanyakumari district.

(ii) To measure the level of growth in fishnet units in Kanyakumari district.

(iii) To observe the relationship between the growth of fishnet units and socio-economic variables related to entrepreneurship in Kanyakumari district.

(iv) To identify the factors promoting growth in fishnet units in Kanyakumari district.

(v) To study the problems faced by fishnet units in Kanyakumari district and to offer suggestions to solve them.

HYPOTHESES

The following are the hypotheses formulated and tested in this study.

Ho_1 : There is no significant difference in growth among fishnet units run by entrepreneurs belonging to fishermen and non-fishermen communities in Kanyakumari district.

Ho_2 : There is no significant difference in growth among owned units, hired units and leased units in fishnet industry in Kanyakumari district

Ho_3 : There is no significant difference in the growth of fishnet units owned by entrepreneurs belonging to different religions.

Ho_4 : There is no significant difference in the growth of fishnet units floated by entrepreneurs with different purposes.

Ho_5 : There is no significant difference in the growth of fishnet units producing different varieties of products.

Ho_6 : There is no significant difference in the growth of fishnet units having different sizes of investment in owned capital.

Ho_7 : There is no significant difference in the growth of fishnet units using different numbers of machineries.

Ho_8 : There is no significant difference in the growth among the fishnet units having different number of shifts.

Ho_9 : There is no significant difference in the growth of fishnet units among the fishnet units established during different periods.

Ho_{10} : There is no significant difference in the growth of fishnet units established under different forms of ownership

OPERATIONAL DEFINITION OF CONCEPTS

COAST

The coast is defined as the part of the land adjoining or near the ocean or its salt water arms[35].

FISHING

Fishing is a general term covering the capture of a wide variety of marine and fresh water animals for direct use as food or for derived products.

FISHING SEASON

Fishing goes on, all round the year. But from the stand point of catch, the year may be divided into two seasons, the active and slack. The season may also vary from place to place. In Kanyakumari district active season extended from July to December when fish is caught plenty. The slack season is from January to June.

WEDGE BANK

The wedge bank is a fertile fishing area found in the sea where rich marine biological diversity occurs. Wedge bank may also be defined as a place of marine environment where fish and other food organisms are available in plenty. The water depth of this region is low. The wedge bank was being exploited by the vessels of other countries like Srilanka, Thailand, South Korea and Taiwan. In view of the bilateral agreement between India and Srilanka reached in 1974, one of such wedge bank falls within the territorial water of India. Throughout the maritime countries of the world there are about twenty such wedge banks. Of these one is situated near Cape Comorin (British name for Kanyakumari) the coastline of Kanyakumari district on the eastward as well as westward region about 30 km[36].

FISHING GROUND

Fishing ground is commonly applied to an area in which fishing is carried on. Fishing ground is referred to as continental shelf. It is subdivided into three:

(i) shore area — ranges up to 20 metres

(ii) off shore area — area from 20 metres up to 80 metres

(iii) deep sea area — area beyond 80 meters.

FISHERMAN/FISHER-FOLK

Fisher-folk are one whose primary occupation is fishing and who receives more than 50 per cent of annual income from fishing.

FISHERY

Fishery is an unit engaged raising and/or harvesting fish which is determined by an authority or other entity. Typically the unit is defined in terms of the following: people involved, species or type of fish, area of water or seabed, method of fishing, class of boats and purpose of activities[37].

FISHING GEAR/FISH NETS

Gears are the instruments used for fish catching and the craft provide platform for the fishing operation carrying the crew and fishing gear. Several types of craft and gear are operated in the sea and inland water bodies. Some gears can be operated without the aid of craft. Crafts and gears used in the different parts of the country are mostly indigenous, non-mechanised and locally built. There are different types of fishing gears. They are Gillnet, Shore seine, Trawler net, Driftnet, Set net, and Hooks and lines. Apart from these, there are specific varieties of nets used for catching specific categories of fish. They are Shrimp net, Lobster net, Crab net, Bag net and Saradane net.

FISHING CRAFTS

Fishing vessels or boat equipped for or engaged in searching for, catching, processing or transporting fish or other marine organisms are called fishing crafts. Fishing craft is a platform on which the fishermen sail to and from the fishing grounds, haul their gear, keep the catch and process them. Fishing crafts in use throughout the country are indigenous, non-mechanized and locally built, designed to suit local conditions.

MONOFILAMENT YARN

Monofilament means a single filament which is strong enough to function alone as a yarn, without having to undergo further processing. Transparent PA monofilament is used as single filament for fine gillnets. Monofilaments have large diameter, stiffness and wiry character. They mostly have a circular cross-section with diameter between 0.1 mm or more, but mono filament with oval or flat cross-section are also manufactured with diameter varying from 0.17 to 35 mm. There is no standard term for this type of yarn[38].

MULTIFILAMENT YARN

Multifilament yarn has a silk-like appearance. It is produced in various degrees of thickness, generally much thinner than 0.05 mm diametre. The first type of this filament of a length of 1000 meters weighted less than 0.2 gram and was even thinner than natural silk. Another type of filament having a length of 1000 meters measures weight ranges 0.6 gram to 3 grams. In a multifilament yarn, more than one filament is twisted together[39].

SINGLE KNOT

In a single knot net, either two or more mono/multifilament fibres are knitted together through a single knot.

DOUBLE KNOT

In double knot net two or more single filament/multifilament fibres are knitted together through a loop making action twice to form a double knot.

MESH SIZE

Normally mesh Sizes are represented by "mm". The size starts from 10 mm to 80 mm and up to the maximum mesh size of 320 to 500 mm depending upon the capacity of the machinery.

MECHANISED BOAT

A fishing craft of about 29 to 60 feet in length, made of steel, usually fitted with engines for propulsion, mechanised devices for handling gear and other facilities for enhancing fish catch and for preservation of fish. It is operated normally in offshore waters. These crafts are away from home bases for a period ranging from one week to 3 months, depending upon the length of the craft and nature of fishing.

MOTORISED CRAFT

A traditional fishing craft about 24 to 30 feet in length, made of wood or plywood or fibre-resined plywood, visually fitted with in-board engines or out-board motors for propulsion only but without facilities for enhancing fish catch and for preservation. They operate in coastal waters. These crafts undertake trips, the period of which is usually a day or two.

TRADITIONAL/NON-MECHANISED/NON-MOTORISED/ARTISANAL CRAFT

A primitive and conventional country type fishing craft made of wood, without any mechanical facilities for enhancing fish catch, propulsion or for preservation and operated in coastal waters. These traditional crafts, which undertake daily trips, are of different types each varying in length and shape. The most common types of traditional craft found in the study area use catamarans and shore country craft.

METHODOLOGY

The present study on "Growth of fishnet industry in Kanyakumari district" is an empirical study based on the survey conducted through census method among the fishnet units functioning in Kanyakumari district. The primary data relating to the fishnet units functioning in Kanyakumari district have been collected through a pre-structured questionnaire prepared by the researcher.

The secondary data relating to growth of fishnet industry have been collected from various journals, bulletins, magazines, books, periodicals, unpublished documents maintained in the District Industrial Centre (DIC), Nagercoil and different offices of the Government of India.

A number of discussions had been held with the officials and members of the Fishnet Unit Owners Association in Chennai and Kanyakumari district, and officials of the District Industries Centre (DIC), Nagercoil. The outcomes of the discussions have been appropriately used in the study.

CONSTRUCTION OF TOOLS AND PRE-TESTING

The researcher has devised a pre-structured questionnaire for collecting primary data. The questionnaire was finalised after a pilot study. The pilot study was conducted by interviewing a selected number of entrepreneurs of fishnet units in Kanyakumari district. These interviews helped the researcher to identify the variables to be included/excluded in the questionnaire.

Having identified the variables, the researcher prepared the final questionnaire. The draft questionnaire was then revised in the light of the suggestions and criticisms made by the research supervisor and the fellow researchers. The questionnaire so drafted was circulated among 10 research scholars for a critical review with regard to wordings, format and sequence. In the light of the suggestions, the questionnaire was re-drafted.

The re-drafted questionnaire was pre-tested with 10 entrepreneurs of fishnet units functioning in the study area. The suggestions and comments of the entrepreneurs were incorporated in the questionnaire and the final draft was prepared.

SAMPLING DESIGN

The researcher has adopted census method for collecting data from fishnet industrial units for the study. The list of respondents to be surveyed was prepared from the list of fishnet units registered with the District Industrial Centre (DIC). There are 114 fishnet units functioning in Kanyakumari district which have registered with the DIC. Out of them, only the units which are functioning for the last 10 years in Kanyakumari district have been covered in the study. Out of the 114 fishnet units, only 87 units have positively responded and the rest have either a short period of survival of less than 10 years or have not responded. Hence the study was limited to 87 fishnet units.

GEOGRAPHICAL AREA OF THE STUDY

The study on the growth of fishnet units is conducted in Kanyakumari district which is one of the smallest districts in Tamil Nadu. Kanyakumari district is located on the southern most part of Tamil Nadu having an area of 1684.00 km^2. The district lies between 77° 15′ and 77° 36′ of the eastern longitude and 8° 03′ and 8° 35′ of the northern latitude. This district is surrounded by Tirunelveli District in the North and North East, Kerala state in the North West and the confluence of the Arabian Sea in the West, the Indian ocean in the south and the Bay of Bengal in the East.

Kanyakumari District, once known as the granary of Travancore, lies at the south western Peninsula. It was in Travancore (Kerala) for a long time and then merged with Tamil Nadu in 1956 under the State Linguistic Re-organization Act. It is famous for its vast green stretches of paddy fields, rich forests, and coconut groves and mineral sands. The district has many beautiful spots.

The coast line is almost regular except for some points of land projecting into the sea at Cape Comorin. There are minor ports in the district at Colachel, Thengapattinam, Manakudy, Kovalam and Arockiapuram. The headquarters of the district is Nagercoil. The district is divided into two revenue divisions namely Padmanabhapuram and Nagercoil having the head quarters at Thuckalay and Nagercoil respectively. There are four taulks namely Vilavancode, Kalkulam, Agateeswaram and Thovalai. This district has four municipalities namely, Nagercoil, Padmanabhapuram, Colachal and Kuzhithurai and nine Development blocks. Six blocks namely Melpuram, Munchirai, Killiyoor, Thiruvattar, Thuckalay and Kurunthencode form the part of Padmanabhapuram revenue division and the remaining three, Agasteeswaram, Rajakkamangalam and Thovalai come under Nagercoil Development Division. There are 56 special village panchyats in this district.

Population

As per 2001 census, Government of India the district has a population of 16, 69,763 with 8, 29,542 males and 8, 40,221 females. The density of population in this district is 992 per sq km while that of the whole country is 324 and the State of Tamil Nadu is 478 per square kilo metre. The availability of the basic infrastructural facilities has attracted many small scale industries like cashew and net making and a few medium scale industries like cotton mills. Yet the district continues to be backward in industrial development and entrepreneurial effort[40].

Education

The district is literally advanced with a literacy rate of 87.6 per cent. This district has one Government medical college, one private medical college, 16 private Arts Colleges, 7 private Engineering colleges, one Government engineering college and 8 polytechnic colleges, one Government polytechnic, 122 higher secondary schools and 120 High schools. The prevailing academic atmosphere in the district helped to achieve 87.6 per cent literacy in this district[41].

Tourist Attraction

Kanyakumari, the land's end, located at the southern most end of India, attracts tourists from other states of India and even from foreign countries. The Gandhi Mandapam, Vivekananda Rock Memorial, Thiruvalluvar statue of 133 feet height in sea, Kamaraj Manimandapam, Bahavathi Amman temple, Suchindram temple, Vattakottai, Padmanabhapuram palace with an archaeological museum, Mandaikadu Bagavathi Amman temple, St. Xavier's church Kottar, Mosque at Thuckalay, Pechipparai and Perunichani dams, Thiruparappu water falls, Ulakkai Aruvi, Changudurai and Chothavilai beaches and Muttom are the important places of attraction for tourists in the district[42].

The congenial climate attracts both Indian and foreign tourists, to Kanyakumari district. Marunthuvalmalai attracts spiritualists seeking solace in solitude. Kodayar hydel project is a power generating scheme housed in the district. It is supplemented by a number of windmills in Aralvoimozhy of this district.

Industries in Kanyakumari district

Kanyakumari district had no major industries in the past. However, now there are a variety of small scales and cottage industries located at different parts of the district provide opportunity for entrepreneurship. At present, the Indian Rare Earth Ltd. at Manavalakurichi and the Spinning mills at Nagercoil and Aralvoimozhi and the Vijayalekshmi Cashew Company at Palavilai are the four major industries in this district. Indian Rare Earth Ltd. (IRE) is a major large scale industry located in Kanyakumari district.

Large Scale Industry: The Travancore Minerals Limited, a private company established their Mineral unit at Manavalakurichi which was taken over by the Government of India and named it as the Indian Rare Earth Ltd. It separates the various components of the sand, the most important is monosite which contains approximately 9 per cent thorium and 0.3 per cent uranium. Among the other commercially valuable components separated, the most important one is ilmenite, which serves as a valuable raw material, in various industries. Zircon is the other commercial product which is principally used in the manufacture of high temperature refractors. All of these products have a good export market. The factory produces 72000 metric tones of ilmenite, 5000 metric tones of zircon, 5000 metric tones of Garnet, 4000 metric tones of Monosite 15000 metric tones of Rutile 300 metric tones of sillimanite, 10 metric tones of Zirconium Oxide and 2 metric tones of Zirconium Oxychloride annually.

Cashew Kernal Processing Industry: As a foreign exchange earner cashew processing industry has a distinct place in the industrial map of Kanyakumari district. There are 171 small scale cashew processing industries in the district. Of the total quantity handled by them, 92 per cent cashew nuts (raw) are imported from East Africa and the remaining 8 per cent are purchased from the local market.

Cottage Industries: *Cotton Handloom* — There are 13,157 looms in this district. Of which, 11531 looms are in the co-operative fold. There are 70 weavers' co-operative societies and the percentage of co-operative coverage is 87. The bulk of the production of handloom fabrics consists of dhotis and towels. Handloom Co-operative Societies located at Vadaseri in Agasteeswaram taluk produces handloom goods which are popular throughout the State.

Coir Industry: Coir Industry is carried on along the coastal areas from Cape Comorin in the south to Kollencode in the north west. About 95 per cent of the coir produced in the district is sent to places outside the district. There are 42 co-operative coir societies functioning at present. The Government coir training school located at Eathamozhi, trains workers in coir making.

Honey Processing: The Young Men's Christian Association (Y.M.C.A.) Rural Reconstruction Centre at Marthandam is engaged in bee-keeping. The centres collect honey from individual bee-keepers and market it under their banner. The honey gathered here is sent to other parts of the State.

Household industry: Household industry absorbs 4.47 per cent of the total working force. There are 34,260 persons employed in household industry in Kanyakumari district as per 2001 census.

The abundant supply of raw materials like rubber, tapioca, palmyrah products, bamboo woods of all kinds, coconut products and the like promote both large scale and small scale industries in the district. It is worth mentioning that rubber industry and coir industry are in the forefront in this district. The industrial estate at Nagercoil and Industrial colony at Kaapikadu near Marthandam are the two industrial centres established by the Government for industrial development in the district. Formation of a rubber park at Shenbagaramanputhur is at the active process of the government of Tamil Nadu.

PERIOD OF THE STUDY

The primary data relating to 10 years from 1999 to 2008 were collected for this study from the fishnet units in Kanyakumari district, which have been used for the study.

FIELD WORK AND COLLECTION OF DATA

Field work for the study was carried out by the researcher. It was conducted during the period of one year from March 2007 to February 2008.

The researcher used the specially devised questionnaire for the collection of data from the fishnet units in Kanyakumari district. The filled up questionnaire were checked and edited. The omissions and commissions in the questionnaire were either rectified on the spot or through revisit. It made the researcher to visit the entrepreneur once again.

DATA PROCESSING

After the completion of the data collection, the filled up questionnaire were edited properly to make them ready for coding. Then the collected data were coded and transcribed on transcription cards. With help of the transcription cards, classification tables were prepared. The classification tables were used for further analysis.

Secondary data published in various journals, bulletins, magazines, technical books, periodicals, unpublished documents maintained in the District Industries Centre, Nagercoil, statistical information published by the Government of India and the official documents of Fishnet Manufactures Association have also been appropriately used.

MEASUREMENT OF THE VARIABLES AND FRAMEWORK OF ANALYSIS

The analysis is made with the help of the classification tables, ratios and other statistical tools keeping in view the objectives of the study. Growth of fishnet units has been analysed in terms of ten variables. They are:

(i) Gross profit
(ii) Net profit
(iii) Production Capacity
(iv) Production Capacity
(v) Sales
(vi) Capacity Utilised
(vii) Number of Employees
(viii) Assets Owned
(ix) External Liabilities
(x) Raw materials Utilised

The extent of growth in fishnet units in Kanyakumari district has been analysed with the help of Multiple Discriminant Analysis. The Batacharya model has been employed to measure the level of growth in fishnet units in Kanyakumari district. 'Z' values were calculated, for each fishnet unit using Batacharya model.

Several accounting ratios as used in the Batacharya model were employed in the study. The accounting ratios used in the study are:

(i) Working capital to total asset
(ii) Return on capital employed
(iii) Gross profit/loss to total asset
(iv) Net worth to Total liabilities
(v) Sales to Total asset.

Industrial units with 'Z' score below the first critical value are referred to as low growth units. The units with 'Z' score above the second critical value are noted as high growth units. This criterion is employed for all the 87 units selected in the study. Thus all the fishnet units are categorized into two groups on the basis of their level of growth - Growth units and Non-growth units. The level of growth has been individually calculated for the last 10 years. The tendency of growth has been measured through Compound Growth Rate. The tendency of growth helped to analyse the level of growth among the fishnet units in Kanyakumari district.

STATISTICAL TOOLS USED

Various statistical tools employed in the study for analysis are:

Compound Growth Rate (CGR)

Compound Growth Rate is a statistical tools employed to measure the growth of a variable over a continuous period of time. The base year value is denoted as y (t = 100) i.e. 100 if it is assumed that it grows over a time at the rate of 10 per cent (or any other rate) every year then the values of *y* at different years are:

Period	Y	Equivalent to
t = 0	100	$100(1+.1)^0$
t = 1	100+10 = 110	$100(1+.1)^1$
t = 2	110+11 = 121	$100(1+.1)^2$
t = 3	121+12.1 = 133.1	$100(1+.1)^3$
......	......	......
t = t	......	$100\ (1+.1)^t$

Therefore the general expression for growth series can be

Yt = $Y_0\ (l+g)^t$

= ABt where Y_0= A and (l+g) =B

@ Yt = AB^t

Taking log both the sides

Log Yt = log A+t log B

i.e. Y* = $A^* + t\ B^*$

When log Yt = Y^*

Log A = A* and log B = B*

It is a simple regression line in Y* and t. B* can be estimated using least square method. Then the estimated compound growth rate is obtained as $\hat{g}$ = [(Antilog * $\hat{B}$)-1].

For expressing the compound growth rate in percentage $\hat{g}$ is multiplied by 100. That is,

$100\ \hat{g}$ = [Anti log $\hat{B}$ * -1]*100

Thus Compound Growth Rate is calculated as Formula

$$\hat{B}^* = \frac{\Sigma Y^*t - \frac{(\Sigma y^*)(\Sigma t)}{N}}{\Sigma t^2 - \frac{(\Sigma t)^2}{N}}$$

Multiple Discriminant Analysis

The Multiple Discriminant Analysis is a multi variate analysuis discriminating the variables into different groups. In multiple discriminant analysis, a separate discriminant function is formed for each pair of groups. Thus, if there are three groups to be formed, there are three discriminant functions [(3) (3-1)] ÷ 2. The coefficients of variables (beta values) in each function shall indicate the importance of the variables for discriminating between the pair of groups. The D score for each discriminant function shall indicate the group to which individual/item shall be more likely to belong.

Linear discriminant function is a linear function of predictive variables weighted in such a way that it will discriminate among groups minimising the error. In case the dependent variable is classified into only two groups, this is taken as simple discriminant analysis. However, in case the dependent variable is classified into more than two groups then this is termed as multiple discriminant analysis. The linear discriminant function for classification into two groups, considering several discriminating (independent) variables, is expressed as:

$$D = b_1x_1 + b_2x_2 + \ldots + b_kx_k$$

where,

$b_1, b_2 \ldots b_k$ = Discriminant coefficients of 1 2 3 . . . k variables

D = Discriminant score for classification of individual/items.

The basis of classification of individuals/items is:

If $D > D_{crit}$, the individual item to be classified as belonging to group I.

If $D < D_{crit}$, the individual item to be classified as belonging to group II.

In simple discriminant analysis, thus, the individuals are classified into either group I or group II, depending upon their discriminant scores (D).

D_{crit} = Critical value or a discriminant score.

Chi-square Test

Chi-square test 'χ^2' is a non-parametric test used to test the goodness of fit of a variable. It is also used to test whether the deviation between observation (experiment) and theory is due to chance (fluctuation of sampling) or it is really due to the inadequacy of the theory to fit the observed data.

Chi-square test starts with a null hypothesis that there in no significant difference between the observed (experimental) and the theoretical or hypothetical values. Karl Pearson the propounder of Chi-square test[43] proved the statistic is

$$x^2 = \sum_{i=1}^{n}\left[\frac{(0_i - E_i)^2}{E_i}\right]$$

i.e.

$$= \frac{(0_1 - E_1)^2}{E_1} + \frac{(0_2 - E_2)^2}{E_2} + \ldots + \frac{(0_n - E_n)^2}{E_n}$$

Where,

df = (c - 1) (r - 1)

01, 02, . . . On = Observed frequencies

E_1, E_2, . . . En = Expected or theoretical frequencies[44].

Factor Analysis

Factor analysis is another statistical tool employed to find out the factors responsible for the growth in fishnet industrial units. The factor analysis identified that there are five factors comprising of 21 variables responsible for industrial growth in fishnet units in Kanyakumari district. The identified latent correlating variables are:

1. Availability of raw-materials
2. Infrastructural facilities
3. Uninterrupted power supply
4. Availability of skilled man power
5. Previous experience in the same industry
6. Previous experience in the other industry
7. Locational advantage
8. Family support
9. Type of competition
10. Educational qualification
11. Generation of ownership

12. Communal setting
13. Growth in capacity utilization
14. External liabilities
15. Period of credit allowed
16. Advertisement
17. Export subsidy
18. Expansion of marketing area
19. Usage of advance machinery
20. Asset background of the family
21. Social status

The factor analysis model in matrix notation is given by

$$x = Af + e$$

where,

$x = (x_1, x_2, x_3 \ldots x_p)$

$f = (f_1, f_2, f_3 \ldots f_m)$

$e = (e_1, e_2, e_3 \ldots ep)$

m = number of factors and

p = number of variables

and the matrix is

$$A = \begin{bmatrix} a_{11}, a_{12}, \ldots, \ldots, \ldots, a_{1m} \\ a_{21}, a_{22}, \ldots, \ldots, \ldots, a_{2m} \\ \ldots, \ldots, \ldots, \ldots, \ldots, \ldots, \\ a_{p1}, a_{p2}, \ldots, \ldots, \ldots, a_{pm} \end{bmatrix}$$

Where a_{ij} is factor loadings which give net correlation between the variables x_i and factor f_j (where i = 1, 2, ... p) and j = 1, 2, 3 ... m). It is assumed that the error variable (e) are distributed independently of f and p and e as multi-variate normal distribution.

Multiple Regression

After finding out the factors involved in the growth of fishnet units in Kanyakumari district, the next step is to find out the relationship between the factors and the growth in the study area. 'Multiple regression analysis' has been done to identify the relationship between the factors and the overall growth of fishnet units in Kanyakumari district. The function in log form is as follows:

$$\text{Log } Y = \log b_0 + b_1 \log X_1 + b_2 \log X_2 + \ldots + b_5 \log X_5 + eu$$

where,

Y : Dependent behaviour

$X_1, X_2, X_3, X_4 \ldots X_5$ are independent variables.

$b_0, b_1, b_2 \ldots b_5$ are the parameters of independent variable to be estimated.

b_0 : Regression constant

e_u : error term

In order to test the significance of the estimated parameters, $b_1, b_2 \ldots b_5$, t-test of the following formula is used.

$$t = \frac{b_1}{SEb_i}$$

where,

bi : Parameters of independent variables

SEbi : Standard error of bi[45].

LIMITATIONS OF THE STUDY

The study is heavily affected by lack of adequate primary data because, the fishnet owners are not ready to give accurate information about the units which they run. As there is no agency in India to regulate the functioning of fishnet industry, no secondary data related to fishnet industry is available in the country. So at many places the researcher is handicapped with sufficient secondary data.

SCHEME OF THE REPORT

The present study entitled "*Growth of Fishnet Industry*" has been organised in six chapters.

The *first* chapter titled "Introduction and design of the study" covers introduction, statement of the problem, review of previous studies, scope of the study, objectives of the study, hypothesis, operational definitions, methodology, construction of tools and pretesting, sampling design, geographical area of the study, period of study, field work and collection of data, data processing, measurement of variables and framework of analysis, limitations of the study and scheme of the report.

The *second* chapter, "Fishnet Industry — A Review" starts with an introduction to fishnet industry and explains the details of fishnet industry. It further explains different crafts and gears used in fishing. Technology adopted in fishnet industry is vividly presented in this part. Further, the fishing gears used in India and Tamil Nadu are explained in length. The chapter ends with a brief history of the fishnet units in Kanyakumari district.

The *third* chapter, "Growth of Fishnet Industry" measures the growth of fishnet industry in Kanyakumari district. Multiple Discriminant Analysis helped to divide the fishnet units into growth and non-growth units. Compound Growth Rate (CGR) has provided immense help in this task. Multiple Discriminant Analysis helped to find the 'Z' score values, which is used in the chapter for analysis.

The *fourth* chapter, "Entrepreneurship and Growth in Fishnet Industry" identifies ten important variables of entrepreneurship having relationship with a growth of fishnet units. In order to test the relationship, Chi-square test is applied.

The *fifth* chapter, "Factors Promoting Growth of Fishnet Industry in Kanyakumari district" locates the factors promoting growth. Factor analysis reduces the 21 variables into five factors as influencing growth in fishnet units. All such factors have been discussed in detail in this chapter. The relationship between growth and the individual factors identified by the factor analysis is further analysed through Multiple Regression Analysis.

The *sixth* chapter, "Summary of Findings, Suggestions and Conclusion" gives a full list of findings of the study and put forth suggestions and ends with a conclusion.

REFERENCES

1. Khanna, K.K., Gupta, V.K., *Economic and Commercial Geography*, Sultan Chand & Sons, New Delhi, 1977. p. 61.
2. *Ibid.*
3. *Ibid.*, pp. 6-11.
4. CMFRI, *Annual Report 2003-2004*, Central Marine Fisheries, Research Institute, Cochin, 2004, p. 144.
5. http://www.fisheriesindia.
6. Devaraj, M. Martosubroto, P. *Prospectus and Management of Small Pelagic Fisheries in India*, 1997, RAP Publication, Vol. 31, pp. 91-198.
7. *District Statistical Hand Book*, Department of Economics and Statistics, Kanyakumari District, 2007, pp. 1-19.
8. Census 2001, Government of India, New Delhi, 2001, p. 16.

9. Balakrishnan, K.B., *Diagnostic Study and Rehabilitation Scheme for Fishnet (India) Pvt. Ltd.*, Madras, 1991. (Unpublished), p. 3.
10. www.FAO.com, *Indian Fisheries — Economic Role of the Fishing Industry.*
11. *Op.cit*, p. 5.
12. Mohan Joseph Modayil, *Challenges for Indian Marine Fisheries*, CMFRI, Cochin, 2000, p. 56.
13. *Development Commissioner (Small Scale Industries)*, Ministry of Commerce and Industry, Government of India, New Delhi, 1960, p. 1.
14. Kurien, J., Mathew, S., Entry of Big Business Into Fishing — Its Impact on the Fishing Economy, *Economic and Political Weekly*, 1978, 13(36): 1557-1568.
15. Day, R., *Improvement in Handling, Distribution and Marketing of Fish*, ICSSR Sponsored Project, 1979, p. 38.
16. Bhushan, B., *Technological Changes in Fishing in Kerala*, M.Phil. Dissertation. Centre for Development Studies, Trivandrum, 1979, p. 8.
17. Tendel, *Operational Constraints of Fishermen Along the Karnataka Coast*, SAG Publication, Mumbai, 1981, p. 142.
18. Sreenivasan, *Economics of Various Types of Fishing Crafts Operated in Tamil Nadu*, Marine Fishing Information, CMFRI, Cochin, 1981, p. 94.
19. Kurien, J., *Causes for the Poverty Among the Fishermen*, Self-enforcing Transaction, Reciprocal Exposure in Fisher folk, Oxford University, UK, 1981, pp. 737-749.
20. Advani, A.H., *Small Scale Sector Cracking Up*, Business India No. 18, 1981, p. 79.
21. Sathiadas, R., *Mechanization of Indigenous Crafts with Out-board in Tamil Nadu*, 1982, p. 46.
22. Khakhar, K.K. and Patel, H.C., *Technological Changes and Socio-economic Effects — A Study of Fishermen Community of Sourashtra Region*, ICSSR Sponsored Project, 1984, p. 62.
23. Sathiadas, R., Panikar, S.K.P., *Cost and Earning of Trawlers Operating at Tuticorin Fishing Harbour*, Marine Fishing Information Services, CMFRI, Cochin, 1989, p. 100.
24. Srivastava, U.K. and Dharma Reddy, M., *Impact of Mechanisation on Small Fishermen*, Concept Publishing Company, New Delhi, 1986, p. 38.
25. Bindhyachal, *Economics of the Fish Landing of Mechanised and Non-mechanaised Crafts in Vizahapattinam of the Andhra Coast*, 1987, p. 12.
26. Mathiarjuna, *A Study of Marine Fishing Industry in Tuticorin*, Unpublished Ph.D. Thesis, Madurai Kamaraj University, Madurai, 1989, p. 259.
27. Annamalai and Kandoran, *The Economics of Motorised Traditional Crafts*, Analysis of Technical Efficiency of Fishing Crafts, 1990, p. 129.
28. Pazhani, *Fisheries Finance in Kanyakumari District — An Economic Study*, Unpublished Ph.D. Thesis, Manonmaniam Sundaranar University, 1998.

29. Halkan Eggert, *Technical Efficiency in the Swidish Trawl Fishery for Norway Lobster*, Working Papers in Economic No. 53, Department of Economics, Gateborg University, Norway, 2001, p. 3.

30. Fency Health Reena, S.A. *A Descriptive Study of Fishnet Industry in Kanyakumari District*, M.Phil. Thesis Unpublished, 2001.

31. Sean Pascoe and Lourina Colgan, *The Contribution of Unmeasurable Inputs to Fishery Production: An Analysis of Technical Efficiency of Fishing Vessels in the English Channel*, American Journal of Agricultural Economics, 2002, Vol. 84, pp. 585-97.

32. Sathasivalingom, T., *A Study on Fishnet Industry in Kanyakumari District* (unpublished Ph.D. thesis), December 2002, Manonmaniam Sundaranar University.

33. Antony Raj, P., *Export Trade of Marine Products in India, A Study with Special Reference to Kerala and Tamil Nadu*, 2002, p. 14.

34. Randall Kramer, *Artisanal Fisheries in Malaysia*, Working Paper No. 03, Duke University, 2003, p. 83.

35. *The American Heritage Dictionary of English Language*, Houghton Mifflin Company, Fourth edition, 2000, p.43.

36. www.fisheries.com "Fisheries in Kanyakumari District Profile".

37. Fletcher, W.J. et al., *How to Guide for Wild Capture Fisheries*, National ESD Reporting Framework for Australian Fisheries, FRDC Project, 2002, pp. 119-120.

38. Gerhard Klust, *Netting Materials for Fishing Gear*, 1982, pp. 17-18.

39. *Ibid.*, p. 16.

40. *Travancore Archaeological Report*, Government of Travancore, Thiruvananthapurm, 1925, Vol. 1, p. 163.

41. *Kanniyakumari District: Primary Census Abstract*, Census 2001. Ministry of Home Affairs (Directorate of Census Operations - Tamil Nadu).

42. *Action Plan 2005-06*, District Industries Centre, Nagercoil, 2006, p. 9.

43. Arya, P.P., Yesh Pal, *Research Methodology in Management Theory and Cases*, Deep & Deep Publications Pvt. Ltd., New Delhi, 2005, p. 519.

44. Gupta, S.C., *Fundamental of Statistics*, Himalaya Publishing House, Mumbai, 2007, pp. 18.3-18.4.

45. Donald R. Cooper, Pamela S. Schindler, *Business Research Methods*, TATA McGraw-Hill Publishing Company Ltd., New Delhi, 2008, pp. 574-575.

Fishnet Industry
A Preview

INTRODUCTION

Fishnet plays a vital role in fishing. Fishing is an industrial activity, which is facilitated by many other supplementary industries. One among them is fishnet industry. Fishnet industry supplies fishnet which is the instrument through which fishing is carried out. There are different types of fishnet used for fishing in different countries. Fishnets are made up of variety of nylon twines. In different countries different varieties of nylon twines are used for manufacturing fishnets. As the outcome of technical advancement, fishnets and other catching materials have been modernised. Modernisation of fishnet has increased the efficiency of fishing. Because of the increased efficiency in fishing, India is able to meet its fish requirements. The present chapter examines the origin, growth and development of the fishnet sector in various countries, especially in India. The technology and the processes involved in the manufacture of fishnets are explained in detail in this part. Secondary data collected from newspapers, journals, magazines and other published sources are of immense use in the preparation of the chapter. Materials retrieved from internet in different web sites and e-journals have enlightened the researcher to present the chapter in a lucid form. Friendly and official discussions with different authorities in the fisheries department and fishnet industrial units have been of much use to elicit data related to fishnet production.

FISHING

Fishing is the physical activity of catching fish in sea or water ponds. Fishing techniques include netting, trapping, angling and hand gathering. Fishing is one of the oldest industries in the world. Indian fisheries sector has considerable economic importance in view of its resources potential, employment opportunities and export earnings. Fishing is an important industrial activity which supplies fish that has become a regular food for more than 50 per cent of the people in India. Further, the export of fish from the country earns a considerable foreign exchange to the exchequer of the country. In recent years, fisheries sector has made rapid progress in terms of production, income and exports. Further, it is poised to enter the crucial phase of augmented fish production, which would ultimately bring "Blue Revolution" to India, both in marine and inland systems. In the growth of fishing, the role of fishnet, the fishing gears are as important as fishing crafts (vessels).

FISHNET INDUSTRY — A PRELUDE

In fishing the gears and crafts used for fishing assume a major role. Because, the efficiency of fishing depends upon the type of fishing gear (fishnet) and the type of fishing crafts (vessels). Fishnets have been used by fishermen in India from time immemorial. Traditionally fishnets were made up of cotton yarns. In those days fishnets were manually made by hand from cotton yarns. It is not cost and time efficient. Further, the volume of catch made by the traditional fishnets was also very low. It made to modernise fishnet making. Now, due to technological advancement, synthetic (nylon) threads and fibres are used to make fishnets. The synthetic yarns manufactured through machines are used to make high quality nets which are capable of harvesting large volume fish catch. The usage of synthetic yarns also facilitated deep sea fishing. Thus, modernisation in fishnet industry has transformed the fishnet making process cost and time efficient. In brief, the fishnet manufacturing sector has now turned into highly profit oriented one. Hence, now one could notice the entry of many more potential entrepreneurs in this sector. Even many multinational and global corporates to enter in the field.

Fishnet industry is a supplementary one to fishing sector. Modernisation of fishnet industry made the fishing sector very attractive. Fishnet industry comprises of two major sub-sectors. The first one is making of fibre (nylon filament), which is used as the raw-material for fishnet making. There are many industrial units exclusively manufacture nylon yarns and supply the same to the other sector. The other sub-sector in fishnet industry is fishnet making. The units falling under this group purchase fibre (nylon filament) from fibre making units and use it as raw material to manufacture different types of net. Thus, industrial units falling under fishnet industry may either produce the fibre (nylon filament) required for fishnet manufacturing or produce the final fishnet. There are some other units which produce both fibre (nylon filament) as well as the fishnet. These units either sell the fibre (nylon filament) in the market or use it for their own requirement for fishnet making. Sometimes, these units sell their excessive production of fibre in the market. Hence, many units which have started their career with filament making ended with fishnet making. Similarly, many other units started to manufacture fishnets alone have diversified their activities tó produce nylon filament too. Fishnet industry as a major industrial sector includes both the units making yarn (filament) and the units making fishnet. Beyond this, there are foreign companies who also supply nylon yarns and fishnets required for fishing in India.

Fishnet manufacturers have been spread all over India. However, concentration of fishnet units could be noticed in Mumbai, Kolkatta, Hyderabad, Chennai and Kanyakumari. The support extended by the Government has motivated many more new entrants to start fishnet manufacturing units in other parts of the country also. Hence, in recent times many more entrepreneurs have started their career in fishnet making.

ORIGIN OF FISHNET INDUSTRY

There is no historical evidence to trace the origin of fishnet industry either at the global level or at the national level. The main reason for this is that there is no formal agency which regulates the sector either globally or at the national level. However, there are traces in the history to prove that ancient Egyptians used implements for fishing. These are illustrated in the tombs as sceneries, drawings and papyrus documents of Egypt[1]. Similarly there are evidences in the history that the ancient river Nile was full of fish and fishing was carried out by the people around them. During those days the fresh and dried fish were the food for much of the population living around the river Nile[2]. People living in that area used traditional implements for fishing and had fish as their meal. Similarly, there are evidences in the Holy Bible as that during the period of Lord Jesus, there were fisherman who carried out fishing as their profession.

In India, the Pandyas the classical Dravidian Tamil kings were known for the pearl fishery as early as the 1st century BC. There are citations in the Ramayana as that Guha, a boatman who assisted Rama in transporting from one side of the Ganga to the other side, offered fish to Lord Rama as his offering. The sea port Tuticorin was known for deep sea pearl fishing and pearl trade.

The Matsyafed net factory is the pioneering fishnet industry in India[3]. It was established in the year 1966 at Ernakulam in Kerala. This factory used the latest Japanese technology for producing high quality nets to the fishermen. When it was established, it was considered as the largest fishnet company in India. The factory manufactured all types of nets, such as gill nets, trawl nets, and seine nets used in the fishing industry. It also made nets for other applications like bird control in agriculture. The factory produced high quality nets using nylon multifilament and monofilament fibres.

FISHING CRAFTS

Fishing crafts are the navigating instruments used in fishing operation. Fishing craft carries the crew and fishing gears to the sea. It serves as a platform in which the fishermen haul his gear, keep the catch and sometimes process them. There are several types of crafts used in fishing. The types of fishing crafts used in India fall under two general categories. They are non-mechanised and mechanised fishing crafts. The fishing crafts falling under non-mechanised category are catamaran, dugout-canoes, plank built canoes, masula boat and built up boats. The mechanised crafts are line boats, traps boats, dolnetter, gillnetter and trawlers.

The type of fishing craft used depends upon the distance of the fishing area and nature of sea. The crafts used in different parts of the country are mostly indigenous, non-mechanised and locally built. However, mechanised crafts have been introduced in the recent past decades and the indigenous crafts are motorised in large numbers. Table 2.1 shows the details of fishing crafts used in Indian coastal states as on the year 2004.

Table 2.1: Fishing Crafts Used in Indian Coastal States

Sl. No.	States	Traditional Crafts	Motorised Traditional Crafts	Mechanised Boats	Total
1.	Andhra Pradesh	53,853	4,164	8,642	66,659
2.	Goa	1,094	1,100	1,092	3,286
3.	Gujarat	9,222	5,391	11,372	25,985
4.	Karnataka	19,292	3,452	2,866	25,610
5.	Kerala	28,456	17,362	4,206	50,024
6.	Maharastra	10,256	286	8,899	19441
7.	Orissa	10,993	2,640	1,276	14,909
8.	Tamil Nadu	33,945	8,592	9,896	52,433
9.	West Bengal	4,850	270	3,362	8,482
10.	Andaman & Nicobar Islands	1,180	160	230	1,570
11.	Daman and Diu	252	350	805	1,407
12.	Lakshwadweep	594	306	478	1,378
13.	Pondicherry	7,297	505	560	8,362
	Total	**1,81,284**	**44,578**	**53,684**	**2,79,546**

Source: Hand book of Fisheries Statistics 2004. Government of India, Ministry of Agriculture, Department of Animal Husbandry, Dairying and Fisheries, New Delhi, p. 142.

It is clear from Table 2.1 that in terms of total crafts used, Andhra Pradesh ranks first with 66,659 crafts which are followed by Tamil Nadu and Kerala with 52,433 and 50,024 crafts respectively. Andhra Pradesh also ranks first in the usage of traditional crafts which are 53,853 in number. It is followed by Tamil Nadu and Kerala with 33,945 and 28,456 crafts respectively. In the context of motorisation of traditional crafts, Kerala ranks first in India with 17,362 crafts which is followed by Tamil Nadu with 8,592 crafts. It is significant to note that eventhough Gujarat is ranked fourth in terms of the total number of crafts used, it ranks first in terms of the number of mechanised crafts. The total number of mechanised crafts operated in this state is 11,372 which is proportionately large in number among the different types of crafts operated in the state. Tamil Nadu ranks second in operation of mechanised crafts followed by Maharashtra. As a whole, Tamil Nadu, is the state with second highest number of crafts in usage. The popular types of crafts used in Tamil Nadu are non-motorised traditional crafts, motoroised crafts, and mechanised crafts.

Table 2.2 clearly presents the details of the fishing crafts used by fisherfolk in Tamil Nadu in 2005.

Table 2.2: Fishing Crafts in Tamil Nadu

Sl. No.	District	Mechanised Crafts	Motorised Crafts	Non-motorised Crafts	Total Crafts
1.	Thiruvallur	21	2,029	848	2,898
2.	Chennai	642	1,073	276	1,991
3.	Kanchipuram	47	2,009	1,807	3,863
4.	Villupuram	14	914	980	1,908
5.	Cuddalore	970	2,014	1,949	4,933
6.	Nagapattinam	1,984	3,681	3,155	8,820
7.	Thiruvarur	0	101	56	157
8.	Thanjavur	259	400	961	1,620
9.	Pudukottai	764	443	1,540	2,747
10.	Ramanathapuram	1,409	2,009	6,351	9,769
11.	Tuticorin	480	2,984	637	4,101
12.	Tirunelveli	0	1414	279	1,693
13.	Kanyakumari	1,121	3,407	5,392	9,920
	Total	**7,711**	**22,478**	**24,231**	**54,420**

Source: Marine Fisheries Census 2005. Part III (4) Tamil Nadu, Government of India, Ministry of Agriculture, Department of Animal Husbandary, CMFRI, Cochin, p. 340.

Table 2.2 shows the number of fishing crafts used in the various coastal districts of Tamil Nadu. In terms of total crafts used, Kanyakumari district ranks first with 9,920 fishing crafts which is followed by Ramanathapuram district and Nagapattinam district with 9,769 and 8,820 fishing crafts respectively. Nagapattinam district ranks first in using mechanised fishing crafts which is 1,984 in number. It is followed by Ramanathapuram and Kanyakumari district with 1,409 and 1,121 mechanised fishing crafts. Nagapattinam district ranks first in motorisation of fishing crafts (3,681 fishing crafts) which is followed by Kanyakumari and Tuticorin districts with 3,407 and 2,984 fishing crafts respectively. It is significant to note that Ramanathapuram district ranks first in terms of the total number of non-motorisied fishing crafts used in Tamil Nadu. The number of fishing crafts operated in this district is 6,351 which is proportionately large in number among the different types of non-motorised crafts operated, in the different districts of Tamil Nadu. Kanyakumari district ranks second in the use of non-motorised fishing crafts and it is followed by Nagapattinam district.

The fisher-folk of Kanyakumari district use both modern and artisanal fishing crafts. The fishing crafts used in Kanyakumari district are classified into three categories. They are mechanised boats, motorised crafts and non-mechanised traditional crafts.

1. **Mechanised boats:** It is meant for deep-sea fishing. It has facilities to enhance propulsion and fish catch. The different types of mechanised boats in Kanyakumari district are small gillnet boats, trawl boats and shark boats

2. **Motorised craft:** The countrycraft fitted with out-board motor or in-board engines are referred as motorised craft. It includes catamarans, fitted with Lambaradini motors and countrycraft (called 'Vallam' in Vernacular language) made of wood or fibre-resined plywood and fitted with Yamaha or Suzuki engine. These crafts have facilities to enhance propulsion.

3. **Non-mechanised or traditional craft:** It includes shore seines and catamarans. These crafts do not have any facility to enhance propulsion or fish catch.

The distribution of different types of fishing crafts in use in Kanyakumari district for the years 2000 and 2003 are presented in Table 2.3.

Table 2.3 reveals that in Kanyakumari district the number of traditional crafts in use is high with 48.63 per cent and 53.23 per cent of the total number of fishing vessels for the years 2000 and 2003 respectively followed by motorised boats with 38.50 and 31.74 per cent in the respective years. The two main reasons for too much dependence on traditional craft are the low capital cost of vessel and the inheritance of traditional methods of fishing with traditional craft. Another notable feature is that the number of fishing vessels in the district have decreased from 10749 in 2000 to 9179 in 2003 marking a 14.61 per cent decline. The main reason for such a decrease is the reduction in the fishing population in the district due to the increasing rate of educated population and switch over to other jobs.

Table 2.3: Fishing Crafts in Kanyakumari District for the Years 2000 and 2003

Types of crafts	2000		2003	
	Number	Percentage	Number	Percentage
A. Mechanised Boats				
1. Small Gill Net Boats	186	1.73	51	0.56
2. Trawl Boats	759	7.06	811	8.84
3. Shark Boats	438	4.08	517	5.63
Total	**1,383**	**12.87**	**1379**	**15.03**
B. Motorised Boats				
1. Catamarans	480	4.47	1336	14.55
2. Plywood/FRP* country craft (Vallams)	3658	34.03	1578	17.19
Total	**4,138**	**38.50**	**2914**	**31.74**
C. Traditional crafts				
1. Catamarans	5116	47.59	4717	51.39
2. Shore-seines (Country crafts)	112	1.04	169	1.84
Total	**5,228**	**48.63**	**4886**	**53.23**
Grand total	**10,749**	**100.00**	**9179**	**100.00**

Source:

* FRP - Fibreglass Reinforced Plastic.

1. Tamil Nadu Marine Fisher-folk Census 2000. Commissioner of Fisheries, Government of Tamil Nadu, Chennai, 2000, p. 247.
2. Census of Fishing Fleets in Kanyakumari District (Draft Report) 2003. South Indian Federation of Fishermen Societies, Thiruvananthapuram, 2003, p. 14.

FISHING GEARS

Fishing gears include the nets and other supplementary implements used for catching of fish. However, in general parlance, fishing gear implies fishnet alone. There are different varieties of fishnet used for catching fish. Fishnets are made up of synthetic or cotton fibres. Fibres of different dimensions having different specifications, when woven together closely form holes on the surface and finally form the net. The holes on the net (mesh) allow water to pass but arrest the fishes. The fishermen bring the fishnet with them to the sea in the fishing crafts and throw it in the sea and catch fish. Thus, without fishnets, fishing is impossible. The efficiency of fishing to a major extent depends upon the type of fishnet used for fishing. There are different types of nets used for catching different varieties of fish. Specific categories of fishnets are used exclusively for catching specific species of fish. Different types of nets used for fishing have different qualities. The rates of such nets also vary accordingly. The popular fishnets used for fishing are:

CAST NET

Cast net is small round nets with weights on the edges. The fishermen bring it to the sea and throw it on the water. The fishes passing through are caught on the immersed net. The size of the net varies up to four meters (13 feets) in diameter. The net is thrown by hand in such a manner that it spreads out on the water and sinks. Fishes are caught as the net is hauled back in.

GILL NET

It is a fishnet set vertically in the water so that fish swimming into it are entangled by the gills in its mesh. It is a common fishing method used by commercial fishermen in ocean, fresh water and estuary areas. The effective use of gillnet is closely monitored and regulated by fisheries management and enforcement agencies. Mesh size and twine strength, as well as net length and depth are all closely regulated to reduce the catch of non-targeted species.

DRIFT NET

A drift net is a type of gillnet with floats attached to a rope along the top of the net, and weights attached to another rope along the foot of the net. Drift net can range in length from 25 meters (82 feets) to 4 kms (2.5 miles). Nets of up to 50 kms (31 miles) are set in recent times. Since the drift nets are not anchored to the sea bottom and connected to a boat, they are some time lost in storms.

FIXED OR STATIONARY NET

These nets are fixed permanently or temporarily in the tidal zone in the shore water during low tide. The net is fixed at a suitable place by tying it down to wooden poles or stakes which are posted at regular intervals. Sinkers and floats are also used to expand the net increasing the maximum effective catching area. The net may be laid in a single straight line in a zigzag manner. With the high tide, fishes swim to the net and as the tide recedes they get trapped.

DIP NET

These are stationary nets operated from a platform of wooden posts. The net is always placed in a stretched out position. By pulleys and ropes, the net is made to immerse in the water. This net is usually operated during night. Attractive lights are attached to the net, which shine just above the water level. Fishes are attracted by the light and suddenly the net is lifted up and fishes are caught.

TRAWL NET

These nets are also conical in shape and usually towed on the surface or mid waters by powered boats. When it is towed on the surface of the water it is called surface trawl and when it is operated in the mid water or at the bottom it is said to be mid water and bottom trawl respectively.

Bottom trawling

Bottom trawling is a trawling (towing a trawl with a fishnet) along the sea floor. Trawling may be benthic trawling and demersal trawling. Benthic trawling is towing a net at the very bottom of the ocean and demersal trawling is towing a net just above the benthic zone. Bottom trawling has raised issues both from the perspective of environmental concern and sustainable development of fishery. Bottom trawling can destroy sea bed habitats of diverse marine life. Bottom of the sea is the spawning ground of some species. Some countries regulate bottom trawling within their jurisdiction.

Mid-water Trawling or Pelagic Trawling

Bottom trawling can be contrasted with mid-water trawling. In mid water trawling, a net is towed higher in the water column. Mid-water trawling catches pelagic fish such as anchovies, shrimp, tuna and mackerel, whereas bottom trawling targets both bottom living fish (ground fish) and semi-pelagic fish such as cod, squid, halibut and rock fish.

SEINE

A seine is a large fishing net that hangs vertically in the water by attaching weights along the bottom edge and floats along the top. Seine nets are usually long flat nets. It serves as a fence to encircle a school of fish. Boats with seine drive around the fish and encircle it through the net. While hauling the net fishes are caught. Some of the popular types of seines are:

Beach Seines

This is a conical bag like net measuring several hundred feets. One end of the net is tied to a fixed post on the shore while a boat takes the other end into the sea and making a semicircular sweep brings it back to shore. Then,

(a) **Cast Net**

(b) **Hand Net**

(c) **Chinese Net**

(d) **Drift Net**

(e) **Purse Seine Net**

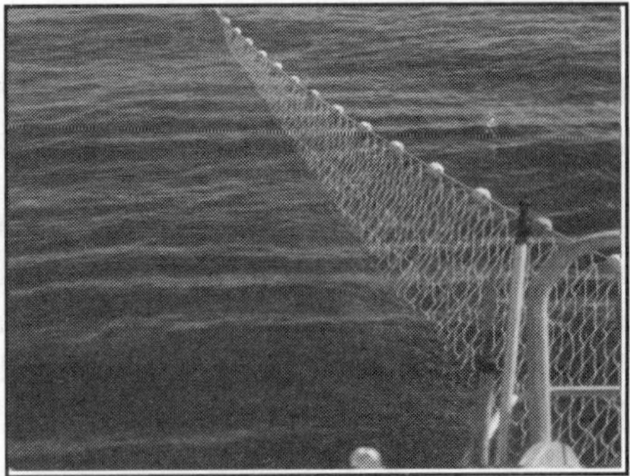
(f) **Gill Net**

Fig. 2.1: **Types of Fish Net**

both the ends are simultaneously dragged to the shore by a group of people. Those fishes that are entangled in the semicircle so purposely made are hauled out and harvested.

BAG NET

Bag nets are conical in shape with a wide mouth and tapering end. Bag nets are used for fishing in fresh water. In running water stream, bag nets are hold against the running water and the fishes passing through caught on the net. In still waters, bag nets are dragged on to catch fish. In sea fishing, bag nets of the large size are hold on by two catamarans on either side of the bag net. By the simultaneous dragging of the bag net by both of the catamarans fishes are caught.

MANUFACTURING TECHNOLOGY

The advent of synthetic fibre is a milestone in fishing gear development. In the early history period, cotton hemp were used for the production of fishnet. Short life and low efficiency in catching ousted the cotton yarns from usage. Modernisation and technological advancement made a revolution in fishnet production technology. Subsequently, different variety of fibres (filaments) came into the scene. Hence then in the place of cotton hemp nylon fibres are used for fishnet making. The non-rotting character of synthetic fibre gained public acceptance in fishnet making, particularly in the tropics.

SYNTHETIC FIBRE (FILAMENT) TECHNOLOGY

Synthetic fibre was introduced around 1920, by Mr. H. Standinger, the Nobel prize winner for chemistry in 1953. He linked all fibre materials consisting of long chain molecules, together to form nylon fibres. Based on this knowledge, additional research has been carried out during the last 50 years, first in the USA, and then Germany, to create such fibre forming macro molecules. As the outcome, nylon fibres were introduced. At present most of the countries manufacture synthetic fibres for different purposes. The countries manufacturing fibres include Japan, the Federal Republic of Germany, the USSR, Great Britain, Italy and France. In spite of the environmental criticisms, wider application of synthetic fibre in many fields made it necessary to continue the commercial production.

SYNTHETIC FISHNET TECHNOLOGY

Synthetic fishnets are made using synthetic fibres. The synthetic fibre used may be monofilament yarn or multifilament yarn. The processes involved in fishnet manufacturing are: (Vide chart 2.1).

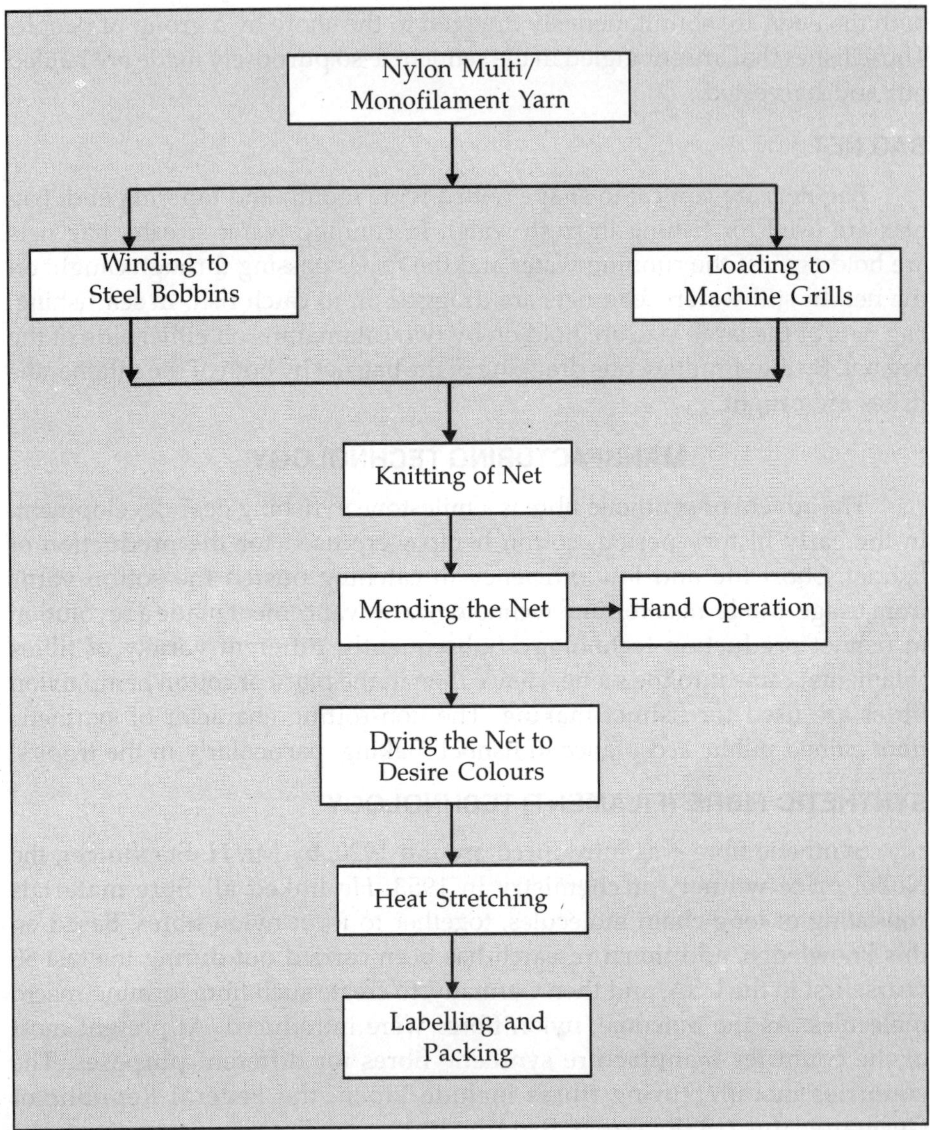

***Chart 2.1:* Fishnet Manufacturing Process**

Threading

Feeding of twines or yarn into the machine is called threading. First the bobbin is loaded with twines or yarns of required dimensions. The bobbins are hung on pegs of the stand of the machine and placed uniformly so as to draw out twines from these spools uniformly. The twines are brought through the warp holes on the two pieces of narrow panel which serves as guide to the twines for making them run parallel to each other. When it is drawn into the machine no loosening of twines should be there. The twines are guided by two coupled uniform supply rolls (rolls covered with wooden cloth). The purpose of this is to adjust the supply of twine from the stand.

Knotting

The twines/yarns are loaded into the machine grills and to the steel bobbins. The winded bobbins are loaded into the bobbin shuttle in the machine, and then the machine will be started. After the twines/yarns are loaded, the machine makes knots in fixed shapes as per the settings. Fishnets are knitted with different number of knots. There are different types of knots. Generally, fishnets are made with either single knot or double knots. The number of knots determines the strength of the net as higher the number of knots lesser the slippage. The number of knots to be made on the net depends upon the mesh size of the net, fishing depth of the sea and other customer specification. Mesh size refers to the hole size of the net which is measured in millimeters. Higher the mesh size higher will be the number of knots. The knots are made in two methods. They are ordinary method and 'U' knot method. The 'U' knot method is similar to 'Tie knot' which is stronger than the ordinary knot and it is used in double knotting only. The distance between the two knots can be 8 mm to 325 mm in accordance with the order received from the customer. After the twines loaded in the bobbins are fully used, the machine stops and the workers replace the empty bobbins with the new one in the bobbins shutters and the knotted net is removed from the machine roller.

NYLON

While nylon was first tested experimentally in the United States of America for gillnets in 1939, there was demand for nylon for military operation in war. It further delayed the development of fibres in fishing industry. But since 1948 the use of nylon in gillnetting has grown rapidly. The superiority of nylon nets over cotton nets are:

(i) Water absorption capacity of nylon is far less than other fibres. It makes handling of net very easy even in very deep water.

(ii) The resistance to knot is the main characteristics of the nylon nets. This property prevents the loss of strength while in use.

(iii) Durability of nylon nets is greater than cotton and hemp nets.

(iv) Nylon nets do not require drying after use.

(v) Nylon net is lighter than any other fibre net of the same mesh size which makes handling easy.

(vi) Even though nylon nets do not require any dying, it can be dyed to give any desired colour according to the marine water colour.

(vii) Nylon nets can be dyed to give any desired colour. It is also suitable for tar-dyeing so that the strength of the net is increased to at least about 20 per cent. It is to be noted that while dyeing the nylon nets, it is necessary to see that it is not boiled, and that the temperature does not exceed 60° C[4].

The change from cotton to nylon nets among professional fisherfolk is practically hundred per cent. They soon realised the great advantage of nylon. Its high catching ability and resistance to rot as compared with cotton were the reasons for the preference of nylon fishnets. Even though there was initial hesitation among the fisherfolk about nylon, in course of time, it was accepted as a good material for fishnet making.

In the manufacturing process of synthetic fibres, the following the steps are undertaken.

First Step

At the first stage the basic raw materials needed for making synthetic fibres are derived from the natural products such as oil, coal, lime and common salt.

Second Step

From the raw materials, the basic substances (monomers) needed to build up the macro-monocles, are obtained by a number of chemical processes. For the production of nylon, two basic substances are needed, namely dipic acid and hexamethylene diamine which are combined with polyamide salt.

Third Step

The third process is polymerization or polycondensation, that is the forming of the chain of macromolecules or polymers. This process consists mainly of heating in an autoclave under high pressure by which, in the case of nylon, a great number of hexane thylenediamine and adipic acid and molecules are alternatively combined together in such a manner that, linear polymers are formed. In the nylon polymers, the two components are linked together by a special atomic grouping known as an amido group. For this reason, polymers of this particular type are called polyamide. The polyamide polymer, the autoclave in the form of ribbons are cut into chips.

Fourth Step

Now the substance polyamide (nylon) is converted into fibre by melting and spinning. For this purpose, the polyamide chips are melted and threads are formed by squirting the molten substance through spinnerets. The viscous thread becomes stiff in air, but they are not yet suitable for use in yarns. They are still extremely ductile and have comparatively low tensile strength.

Final Step

The manufacturing of filaments is finished by drawing the threads that are stretched three to five times of their original length. In the final step, filaments of specified fineness, diameter, tensile strength and extentability attained[5].

Synthetic fibre (nylon filament) was first used for fishing in Japan in 1932. Since then, about 1948 experiments have been carried out on the adaptability of synthetic fibre (nylon yarn) for fishing gear through the co-operation of the fisheries agencies, fisheries colleges, fisheries research institutes, fibre (nylon yarn) makers, fishnet makers and fisher folk[6].

Gillnetting has been greatly benefited by the introduction of synthetic fibre. The requirements of materials for gillnets are fineness, pliability, elasticity, durability and invisibility when used in the water. Polyamide continuous filament yarn are therefore, in great demand for gillnets. It has also been possible to improve the designs of gill nets particularly used in inland fishing.

Nylon yarns produced are of two types. They are monofilament yarn and multifilament yarn.

Monofilament Yarn: In monofilament yarn, single nylon filament is used without any twisting. It is weightless and therefore it is not long lasting. As in the monofilament yarn only one filament is used, they are sold at cheaper prices. The quality of the monofilament yarn depends upon the thickness which is measured by the diameter. In Kanyakumari district filaments are produced with different diameters such as 0.12mm, 0.16mm, 0.18mm, 0.20mm and 0.23mm. Generally, higher thickness (diameter) indicates higher quality and strength of the monofilament yarn. Blending, melting, spinning, cooling, stretching, annealing, oiling, winding and packing are the important stages in the manufacturing of monofilament nylon yarn.

(i) Blending

Nylon chips (phenol made of coal tar) with additive chemicals and dystuff are mixed together with the help of the mixing unit.

(ii) Melting

The mixed raw-materials are put into the hopper of the extruder unit and melted in the cylinder section of the extruder.

(iii) Spinning

In the spinning stage monofilament yarns of specified diameter are extruded through dyes and nozzle plate.

(iv) Cooling

The monofilament yarn is then cooled down at quenching bath where the chilling unit provides the required chilled water.

(v) Stretching

The monofilament yarn is stretched at 4 units so as to achieve the required strength and diametre.

(vi) Annealing

In one of the stretching baths, the stretched monofilament yarn is dried up for annealing.

(vii) Oiling

Any one of the oil is used in this process on the surface of the monofilament yarn, if necessary.

(viii) Winding

The monofilament yarn is wound on the bobbin prepared at each spindle of the take-up winder.

(ix) Packing

Once the monofilament yarn is wound around the bobbin, the bobbins are packed inside a cotton box for delivery and marketing.

Multifilament Yarn (Twine): When two are more filaments are twisted together to form a twine it is known as multifilament yarn. The quality of the multifilament yarn depends up on its size which is counted by the number of filaments twisted. Higher the number of filaments twisted greater is the strength and weight of the multifilament yarn. Generally, the multifilament yarns are produced by twisting two or three nylon filaments. They are represented as 1/2 size and 1/3 size respectively. In the numerical expression, the numerator shows that a single yarn is manufactured by using 2 or 3 fibres.

As the yarns are twisted together, multifilament yarn is otherwise known as twines. Twine is the basic raw-material for fishnet production. Twines are loaded into the machine by way of grills and bobbins. The bobbins are placed in a position to change them by the new one while the machine is running. The quality of the twine is an important factor in determining the quality of the fishnet. If the twine is not of good quality, it often gets cut and it makes more damages in the net. The speed of the machine is also affected by these twine cuts.

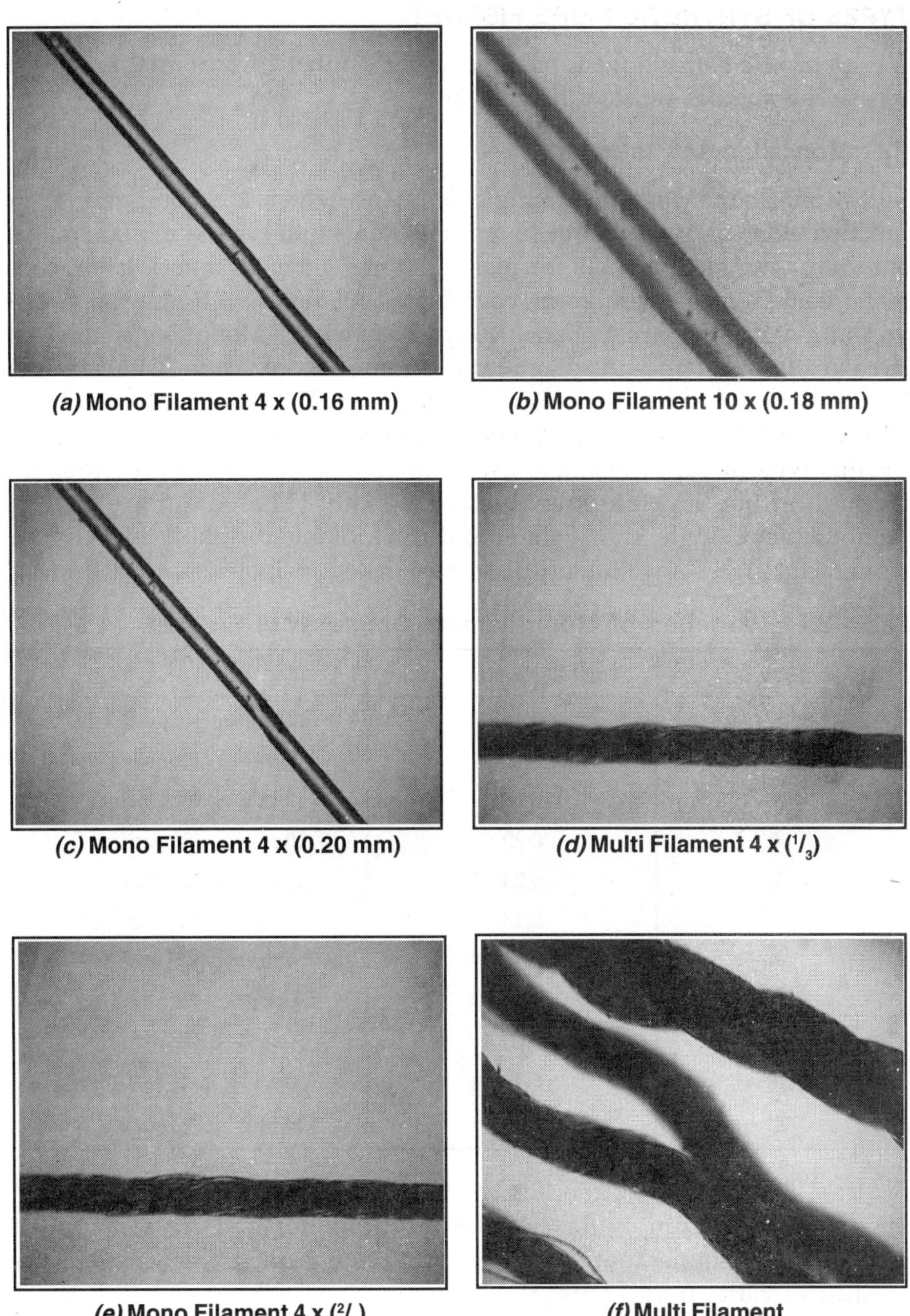

(a) Mono Filament 4 x (0.16 mm)

(b) Mono Filament 10 x (0.18 mm)

(c) Mono Filament 4 x (0.20 mm)

(d) Multi Filament 4 x ($^1/_3$)

(e) Mono Filament 4 x ($^2/_3$)

(f) Multi Filament

Fig. 2.2: Models of Filaments

TYPES OF SYNTHETIC FIBRE FISHNET

Synthetic fishnets manufactured using synthetic fibres are of different types. The popular types of fishnets are:

(i) Monofilament fishnets

Monofilament means a single filament, which is strong enough to function alone as a yarn. Transparent PA (Polyamide) nylon monafilaments are used as single filaments for making monafilament fishnets. In practice, monofilament is a general term, covering all filaments with larger diameter and stiffness and a wiring character (synthetic wires). Monofilaments have a circular cross-section with diameter 0.1 mm or more. Monofilaments with oval or flat cross section are also manufactured. The diameter of such yarn varies from 0.17 mm to 0.35 mm. There are no specific international standards for this type of yarn[7]. Fishnets using monofilaments are knitted together through either a single knot or double knot. The common forms of monofilament single knot fishnet and monofilament double knot fishnet manufactured in Kanyakumari district are listed in Table 2.4 and 2.5.

Table 2.4: Varieties of Monofilament Single Knot Fishnet

Sl. No.	Yarn Diametre (mm)	Mesh size
1.	0.15	12 mm to 300 mm
2.	0.16	12 mm to 300 mm
3.	0.18	12 mm to 300 mm
4.	0.20	20 mm to 325 mm
5.	0.23	20 mm to 325 mm
6.	0.28	30 mm to 325 mm
7.	0.32	30 mm to 325 mm
8.	0.35	30 mm to 325 mm
9.	0.40	50 mm to 325 mm
10.	0.45	50 mm to 325 mm
11.	0.50	50 mm to 325 mm

Source: Primary data.

It is clear from Table 2.4 that the diameter of the yarn used in monofilament single knot varies from 0.15 mm to 0.50 mm. Similarly the mesh sizes varies from 12 mm to 325 mm.

Different varieties of monofilament double knot fishnet are presented in Table 2.5.

Table 2.5: Varieties of Monofilament Double Knot Fishnet

Sl. No.	Yarn Diametre (mm)	Mesh size
1.	0.20	12 mm to 300 mm
2.	0.23	12 mm to 300 mm
3.	0.28	12 mm to 300 mm
4.	0.32	20 mm to 325 mm
5.	0.35	20 mm to 325 mm
6.	0.40	30 mm to 325 mm
7.	0.45	30 mm to 325 mm
8.	0.50	50 mm to 325 mm

Source: Primary data.

It is clear from Table 2.5 that the diameter of the yarn used in monofilament double knot varies from 0.20 mm to 0.50 mm. Similarly the mesh sizes vary from 12 mm to 325 mm respectively.

(ii) Multifilament fishnet

Multifilament fishnet has a silk-like appearance. In a multifilament fishnet, more than one filament is used. It is produced in various degrees of fitness. The filaments used in this fishnet are generally much thinner than 0.05 mm diameter. It is even thinner than the natural silk. This fishnet measuring 1000 meters length weighs between 0.6 gram and 2 grams. All filaments used in this type of net run to the whole length of the yarn. Hence, at every point of cross section the fishnet contains the same number of filaments.

Multifilament fishnets are made through knitting of more than one filament through either a single knot or double knot. Accordingly, the fishnet is either termed as multifilament single knot fishnet or multifilament double knot fishnet. Multifilament single / double knot fishnets are made in various types. The popular sizes of multifilament single / double knots produced in Kanyakumari district are presented in Table 2.6 and Table 2.7.

Table 2.6: Varieties of Multifilament Single Knot Fishnet

Sl. No.	Yarn size	Mesh size
1.	1/2	12 mm to 300 mm
2.	1/3	12 mm to 325 mm
3.	2/2	16 mm to 500 mm

It is clear from Table 2.6 that the nylon filament used in multifilament single knot varies from 1/2 to 2/2. Similarly, the mesh sizes vary from 12.00 mm to 500 mm respectively.

Different varieties of multifilament double knot fishnet are presented in Table 2.7.

Table: 2.7: Varieties of Multifilament Double Knot Fishnet

Sl. No.	Yarn size	Mesh size
1.	2/2	20 mm to 300 mm
2.	2/3	20 mm to 300 mm
3.	3/3	60 mm to 325 mm
4.	4/3	60 mm to 500 mm
5.	5/3	60 mm to 500 mm

It is clear from Table 2.7 that the nylon filament used in multifilament double knot varies from 2/2 to 5/3. Similarly, the mesh sizes vary from 20 mm to 500 mm respectively.

Multifilament nets are made out of multifilament yarns. Multifilament yarns are produced by twisting together two or more filaments. The multifilament nets, both single knot and double knot, vary according to the mesh size and the number of filaments twisted together in making the yarn used. The mesh size in case of multifilament single knot nets ranges from 12 mm to 500 mm whereas in case of double knot nets it ranges from 20 mm to 500 mm. The yarns used in multifilament single knot nets are of three types. In case of the first two types, one monofilament is twisted with a yarn made out of twisting together two monofilaments or three monofilaments. In case of the third type, two yarns made out of twisting together two monofilaments are twisted. All these three types are termed. The yarns used in multifilament double knot nets are of five types. They are termed as 2/2, 2/3, 3/3, 4/3 and 5/3. In case of first type, two yars with two filaments are twisted together and incase of the type '2/3' two yarn with two filaments and three filaments each are twisted together. Similar method is adopted in case of other type also in which, the yarn size represents the number of filaments in the yarns twisted together.

FISHING GEARS IN TAMIL NADU

In Tamil Nadu as in other parts of the country different types of fishnets are used for catching fish. The most popular forms of gears used in Tamil Nadu for fishing are Trawl net, Gill net, Seine net, Bag net, Drift nets and Hooks line. Table 2.4 shows the details of fishing gears used for fishing in various coastal districts of Tamil Nadu as on 2005.

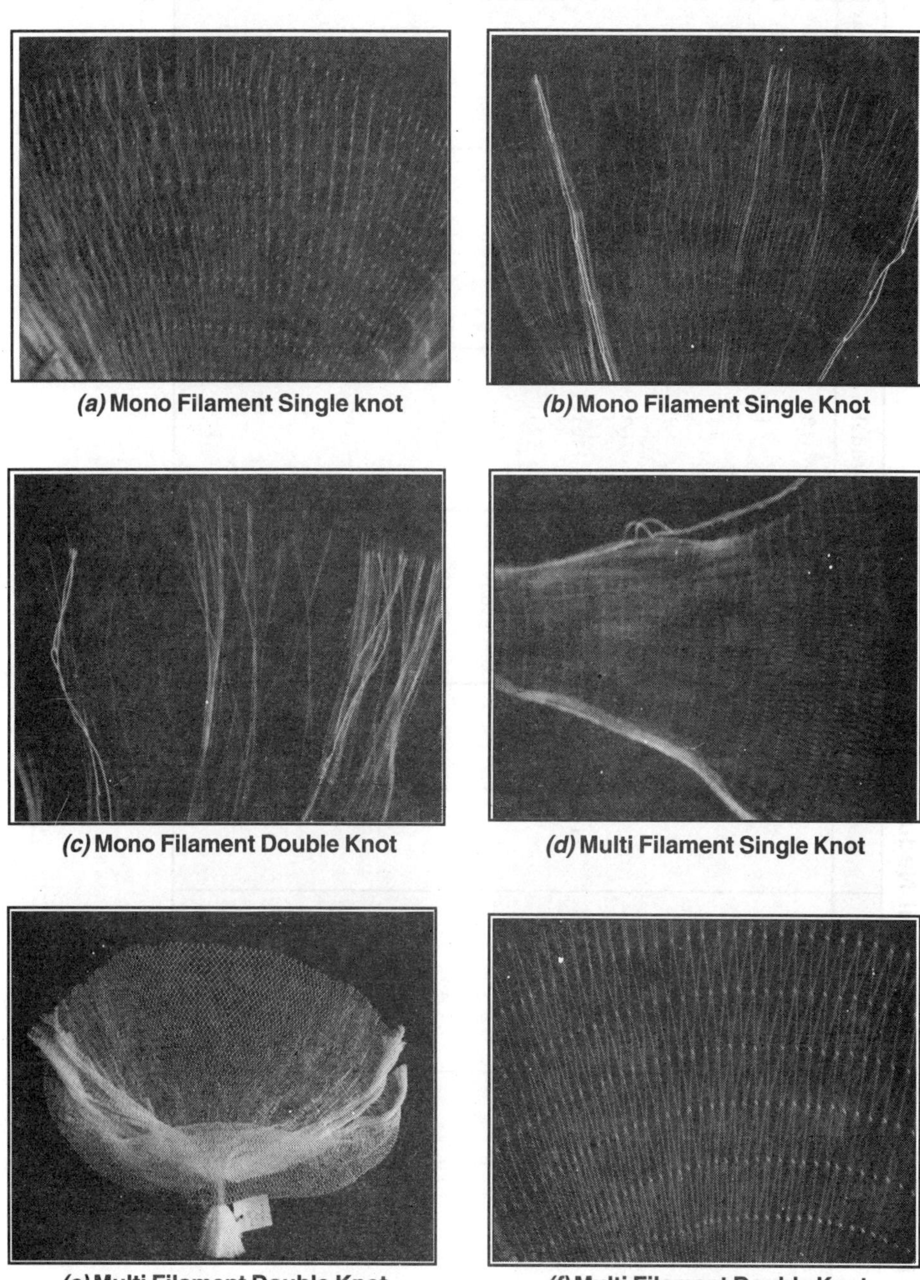

(a) Mono Filament Single knot

(b) Mono Filament Single Knot

(c) Mono Filament Double Knot

(d) Multi Filament Single Knot

(e) Multi Filament Double Knot

(f) Multi Filament Double Knot

Fig. 2.3: **Models of Mono-Multi Single knot and Double Knot Fishnets**

Table 2.8: Fishing Gears Used in Tamil Nadu

District/Gear	Thiruvallur	Chennai	Kanchipuram	Villupuram	Cuddalore	Nagapattinam	Thiruvarur
Trawlnet	41	223	5	8	1180	4239	3
Purse seine	0	0	3	2	44	20	1
Boat seine	0	0	29	1	137	41	0
Fixed bagnet	1	6	638	0	96	76	0
Driftnet	0	112	16	35	2639	0	38
Gillnets	54212	14452	162107	50035	44611	178395	34565
Hooks & lines	4937	570	27847	2370	5931	7656	40
Troll lines	0	8	1387	659	877	689	0
Longlines	1006	523	1296	2160	2181	1687	0
Ring seine	0	1	0	1	7	217	0
Shore seines	0	19	10	16	266	1176	36
Scoop net	4884	706	0	1332	0	0	0
Traps	0	0	0	14	0	0	0
Others	0	0	17	0	743	30	0

(Contd…)

District/Gear	Thanjavur	Pudukottai	Ramanathapuram	Tuticorin	Tirunelveli	Kanyakumari	Total
Trawlnet	675	3508	4655	856	0	1618	17011
Purse seine	0	9	0	0	0	0	79
Boat seine	178	1720	383	108	0	275	2872
Fixed bagnet	243	0	0	0	0	297	1357
Driftnet	1664	99	30875	524	12	691	36705
Gillnets	105375	93982	219200	160909	119133	173999	1410975
Hooks & lines	787	2958	165	8882	190	77736	140069
Troll lines	0	0	45	0	1	8413	12079
Longlines	56	82	241	15292	513	55250	80287
Ring seine	0	0	0	0	0	9	235
Shore seines	1645	1563	545	86	0	328	5690
Scoop net	0	0	0	74	0	827	7823
Traps	0	118	1813	0	0	112	2057
Others	307	1354	23037	0	0	214	25702

Source: Marine Fisheries Census 2005. Part III (4) Tamilnadu, Government of India, Ministry of Agriculture, Department of Animal Husbandary, CMFRI, Cochin, p. 340.

Table 2.8 makes it clear that gillnet is the largely used fishing gear in Tamil Nadu which is followed by hooks and lines and long lines. As per the fishing survey conducted in the year 2005, there were 14,10,975 gillnets used in Tamil Nadu. Ramanathapuram district ranks first in usage of gillnets with 2,19,200 nets which is followed by Nagapattinam and Kanyakumari district with 1,78,395 and 1,73,399 gillnets respectively. Hooks and lines is one of the most commonly used gear by the fishermen especially in Kanyakumari district. Next to Kanyakumari district, hooks and lines are largely used in Kanchipuram district. Long lines are also largely used in Kanyakumari district, which is followed by Tuticorin district. Out of the total 80,287 long lines used in Tamil Nadu, 55,250 are found in Kanyakumari district. Purse seine, ring seine, fixed bag nets and traps are the least used gears in Tamil Nadu. The total number of trawl nets used by the fishermen of Tamil Nadu is 17,011, out of which 4,655 are used in Ramanathapuram district. Ramanathapuram district is followed by Nagapattinam and Pudukkottai with 4,239 and 3,508 trawl nets.

FISHING GEARS IN KANYAKUMARI DISTRICT

Earlier, making fishnet by hand was flourishing as a cottage industry in the coastal villages of Kanyakumari district for a very long time. During that time there was no organised agency to monitor the net making activity. During those days, cotton yarn was used as the raw-material to manufacture fishnet. In course of time nylon or synthetic fibre nets imported from China were used for fishing. But the local fisherfolks were opposing to use such type of nets for fish catching. As nylon has many comparative advantages over cotton yarn, in course of time it got acceptance among the fisher-folk. The efficiency attained in fishing through synthetic fibres positively motivated many other fishers to use synthetic fishnet in the place of cotton fishnets. By the time when there was a great demand for nylon fishnets, both within and outside the district, there were limited number of units in the district producing fishnets. The full demand could not be met by the suppliers. Growing demand for synthetic fishnets made many more new entrants to start fishnet making units in the district. Hence fishnet industry in the district witnessed unexpected growth in 1990's. Since then the sector has been growing by leaps and bound.

Fishnet industry is one of the major small scale industries in Kanyakumari district providing direct and indirect employment to 40,000 people in Kanyakumari district. Mr. Haizar Abdul Majeed of Manavalakurichi is the pioneer for fishnet industry in this district. In the initial years when Mr. Haizer Abdul Majeed started fishnet unit, fishermen were opposing the industry for the reason that mechanisation of fishnet industry would make many of the workers, engaged in fishnet making unemployed. There were dharnas against mechanization of the production of fishnet. So this industry was shifted to Kavalkinaru in Tirunelveli district. But very soon the agitation was amicably settled by the district administration. Hence he shifted back the first nylon fishnet industry to Manavalakuruchi in 1975. Later realizing the prospects and scope of the nylon fishnet industry, Mr. M.C. Balan, Mr. Pon Robert Singh, Mr. F. Stalin, Mr. Nanjil. M Vincent, Mr. Kumaresan and many other prominent entrepreneurs in the district ventured in this business. From 1999, due to the liberalized trade policies of the government, many native entrepreneurs came forward to start fishnet industries. During the period 1990 to 2000 there was a phenomenal growth of fishnet industries in Kanyakumari district.

The fishing gears used by the Kanyakumari district fisherfolk can be classified into six categories — trawl nets, gill nets, shore-seines, hooks and lines, boat-seines and traps. Among the above six groups of fishing gears, there are many sub-groups each meant for capturing specific species of fish. The major fishing gear of the district is fishing net. In 2000 Kanyakumari district accounted for 5.81 per cent of total gears in Tamil Nadu state. Fishing nets constituted 67.09 per cent to state. Fishing nets constituted 67.09 per cent to total gears in the district in the year 2000 followed by hooks and lines with 29.04 per cent. Among the fishing nets, gillnet alone accounted for 6.46 per cent of the total gears[8]. In 2003, the share of fishnet nets, and hooks and lines were 54.61 per cent and 41.81 per cent respectively[9]. The details of fishnet units having registration in the DIC (District Industrial Centre), Nagercoil in Kanyakumari district are furnished in Table 2.9.

Table 2.9: Registered Fishnet Units in Kanyakumari District

Year	Number of Units	Cumulative Total
1990	1	1
1991	1	2
1992	1	3
1993	4	7
1994	7	14
1995	28	42
1996	25	67
1997	16	83
1998	11	94
1999	8	102

(Contd...)

Year	Number of Units	Cumulative Total
2000	3	105
2001	0	105
2002	0	105
2003	2	107
2004	2	109
2005	4	113
2006	1	114
2007	0	114

Source: DIC, Konam, Nagercoil.

It is evident from Table 2.9 that the fishnet industry witnesses a tremendous growth during the period 1995 to 1998. As the outcome, out of the 114 fishnet units presently existing in the district, 69 units representing 61 per cent were established during this period.

In Kanyakumari district, Konam, A.N Kudy, Vellamodi, Erachakulam, Pottal, Paruthivilai, Erumbukadu are the areas where large number of fishnet units are clustered. All the above mentioned places have come under Agesteeswaram Taluk.

SUMMARY

An overview of the fishnet industry presented in this chapter gives a vivid picture about the sector. There are different types crafts and gears used for fishing. The fishnet industry has a long history which dates back to pre-history era. The origin, growth and development of fishnet industry explained in the chapter presents metamorphosis of the industry over years. Fishnets used at different places differ widely. They vary according to the materials used, process of making and the species of fish caught. Fishnet industry is one of the important subsidiary industries in the fisheries sector earning a considerable income to the exchequer of the nation. Introduction of synthetic yarn has transformed the industry from traditional into modernised one. The industry comprises of two major sub-sectors namely manufacturing of filament and fishnet making. Both the sub-sectors of the fishnet industry are equally important. Fishnet industry being one of the small scale industries in Kanyakumari district, having started its journey only after 1975, has achieved a phenomenal growth. Around 40,000 people are directly and indirectly employed. The achievement of the industry in a very short period is incredible.

REFERENCES

1. http://www.newworldencyclopaedia.org/entry. Ocean Net Fishing, Initiative Constitutinal Amendment Sacramento Cali, Election Division, 1987.
2. www.fisherieshistory, Gift of the Nile.pdf.
3. www.FAO: Fisheries and Aquaculture Literature.
4. Small Industry Scheme No. 159, *Nylon Fishing Nets*, Development Commissioner (Small Scale Industry) Ministry of Commerce and Industry, Government of India, New Delhi, p. 283.
5. Gerhard Klust, *Netting Materials for Fishing Gear*, Fishing News Book, London, 1982, pp. 6-10.
6. *Ibid.*
7. Gerald Kulst, *Op.cit.*, pp. 17-18.
8. *Tamil Nadu Marine Fisherfolk Census 2000*, Commissioner of Fisheries, Government of Tamil Nadu, Chennai, 2000, p. 249.
9. *Census of Fishing Fleets in Kanyakumari District (Draft Report) 2003*, South Indian Federation of Fishermen Societies, Tiruvananthapuram, pp. 31-39.

Growth of Fishnet Industry

INTRODUCTION

The growth of a business enterprise depends upon the business environment prevalent at a point of time. Environmental changes on socio-economic, political and environmental variables influence the business. In order to survive in the changed and changing business environment, a business enterprise is needed to be strong enough. This implies that only the business units which have strong growth can sustain in the changed environment. This underlies the need for the growth of business enterprises. Growth is a natural phenomenon and a continuous process in the business. Generally a business enterprise starts in a small way and grows big with the passage of time. In simple terms, growth implies strength and stamina of the business. Growth enables a business enterprise to face challenges, competitions and hardships. Thus growth ensures the survival of the business even in adverse and hard times[1].

In the common parlance, increase in sales, profit and output are identified as the major symptoms of a growing business. Growth means production and sales results in economies in production and marketing. Economics of production and marketing in turn, reduce production cost per unit and increase the profit earned per unit[2]. Hence, the growth of production and sales are assumed as the indicators of growth.

However, those are not alone the variables of growth. There are innumerable variables indicating growth. This chapter deals with the growth of fishnet units in depth in Kanyakumari district. The growth and the extent of growth witnessed by fishnet units are presented in detail in this chapter. The growth of fishnet units in Kanyakumari district is analysed through, ten identified growth factors. It has been measured on the basis of scores awarded to those ten components. Scaling technique has been employed in awarding scores for the growth variables.

Primary data collected through a structured questionnaire is used for the preparation of the present chapter. Secondary data available in the books, journals, newspapers and various web sites have been of immense use in the preparation of the chapter.

CONCEPT OF GROWTH

Growth is a term which does not have any common acceptable definition. Oxford Advanced Learners Dictionary[3] explains 'growth' as 'development' or 'increase'. Growth means, improvement, enhancement, development, forward looking, up-lift and like in the well being of oneself. In other words, the state of growing in size or proceeding to increase to the successive stage is referred as growth.

In business, growth means growing in size in terms of net worth and asset backing, resulting in addition to product line, exploring further markets and the like. Generally business growth is attained at two levels. They are:

(i) At the same level (Horizontal growth)

(ii) At different levels (Vertical growth)

HORIZONTAL GROWTH

Growth at the same level of business, popularly known as horizontal growth, involves the acquisition of one or more competitors. For example, a fishnet unit may grow by acquiring another fishnet unit. The most important advantage of horizontal growth is that it eliminates or reduces the competition.

VERTICAL GROWTH

Growth at different levels is known as vertical growth. Vertical growth may be:

(i) Backward growth, or

(ii) Forward growth

Backward Growth

Backward growth involves starting from the preceding stage of the current business. For example, a manufacturer of a fishnet product may start the manufacture of the raw-materials required for the finished product. For instance, a fishnet manufacturer may take up the manufacture of nylon yarn that is a raw-material for fishnet. Similarly if a company that currently markets the products takes up the manufacturing the same product it is called backward growth.

Backward growth has certain advantages. It ensures smooth supply of materials for production or goods for marketing. This is particularly important when there are supply bottlenecks. Secondly, it enables the company to obtain the goods cheaply or to make profit out of manufaeturing. Thirdly, it also helps the company to ensure quality of goods. Further, it also facilitates tax savings.

Backward growth however is not an unmixed blessing. In some cases it has problems. The cost of making may be higher than the cost of buying.

Forward Growth

Forward growth means entering the subsequent stage of the industry. For example:

(i) The manufacturer of a product who does not do marketing of a product currently may start the marketing of it.

(ii) The manufacturer of the raw- materials may take up the manufacture of the finished product. For instance, yarn manufacturer may start the manufacture of fishnet.

The advantages of forward growth are:

(i) It creates captive demand for the product

(ii) It generates additional profit.

The major risk of forward growth is that there is no guarantee that the new business will be a success.

Diversification is another way to achieve growth. Diversification means adding new lines of business. The new lines of business may be related to the current business or may be quite unrelated. If the new lines added making use of the firm's existing technology, production facilities and distribution channels it amounts to backward or forward growth. It may be regarded as related diversification.

RISK OF GROWTH

It is important to note that there are several risks associated with growth. Growth may land some companies in trouble. Common risks associated with growth are:

(i) An increase in the productive capacity may lead to an adverse effect if the demand falls.

(ii) If the new business fails, it could sometimes even affect the old business.

(iii) There is a tendency to concentrate more on the new business at the expense of old business.

(*iv*) A rapid and substantial growth of business may sometimes lead to an effective management.

(*v*) When a firm becomes large, it may loose several advantages like tax concession, subsidies, exemption from several laws causing an increase in costs and other problems.

(*vi*) As a firm grows significantly it is likely to receive more attention from the competitors and the public[4].

However, the growth is inevitable and essential to a firm to sustain in the field.

GROWTH VARIABLES — INDICATORS OF GROWTH

Growth of an industrial unit is visible on different aspects of functioning of the organization. The unit which has recorded a growth shall have a positive multi-dimensional development. It is difficult to exactly pinpoint all the areas where such a development could be noticed. However, from past experience and observation the following variables are identified to be the leading indicators of growth.

Though the growth is indicated by innumerable variables, significant ones are rarely few. In the study such identified variables alone have been included for analysis. There are ten such variables that have been identified by the researcher as the indicators for growth in fishnet industry. They are:

(*i*) Gross Profit

(*ii*) Net Profit

(*iii*) Production Capacity

(*iv*) Sales

(*v*) Capacity Utilised

(*vi*) Capital Employed

(*vii*) Employees

(*viii*) Assets Owned

(*ix*) External Liabilities

(*x*) Raw materials Utilised

GROSS PROFIT

Gross profit is the difference between sales and cost. Expenses incurred by the firm in the production of goods and services are represented as cost. It includes all direct expenses related to the manufacturing of goods. Sales mean the revenue generated by the firm by selling of finished product in the market. Gross profit tells how much money a business would have made if it did not pay for any other expenses such as salary, income tax and the like. Gross profit ratio, indicates the relationship between gross profit and sales. A high ratio of gross profit to sales is a sign of good growth. It implies that the cost of production of the firm is relatively low. It may also be indicative of a higher sales price without corresponding to the increase in the cost of goods sold. It also shows that the cost of sales might decline without a corresponding decline in sales.

Low gross profit is a danger signal, warranting a careful and detailed analysis of the factors responsible for it. The important contributory factor may be:

(i) A high cost of production reflecting acquisition of new raw materials and other inputs on unfavorable terms, inefficient utilisation of current as well as fixed assets, and so on; and

(ii) A low selling price resulting from competition, inferior quality of the product, lack of demand and so on[5].

In Kanyakumari District most of the fishnet manufacturing units are earning gross profit over years while a few units have shown low gross profit. A few others who have shown low gross profit in the initial years earned considerable gross profit in the later years. Similarly in many other cases, low gross profit making concerns in the initial years have recorded more gross profit in the recent years. It shows that gross profit has been widely fluctuating in different fishnet units over years. In order to analyse the growth of gross profit achieved by fishnet units Compound Growth Rate is used. Compound Growth Rate comprehends the growth of gross profit achieved by different fishnet units in the last 10 years into a single figure. The growth arrived by fishnet manufacturing units in the last 10 years as assessed through Compound Growth Rate (CGR) measures the growth of the fishnet units. The growth of gross profit in fishnet units in Kanyakumari district is presented in Table.3.1.

Table 3.1: Growth of Fishnet Units in Terms of Gross profit

Sl. No.	Growth (in Percentage)	Number of Units	Percentage
1.	(-) 25 – (-) 5	1	1
2.	(-) 5 – 0	45	52
3.	0 – 5	30	34
4.	5 – 10	10	12
5.	Above 10	1	1
	Total	**87**	**100**

Source: Primary Data.

It is clear from table 3.1 that 53 per cent of the fishnet units in Kanyakumari district have achieved a negative growth (no growth) in the last 10 years ending with 2008. Negative growth does not show that the fishnet units are incurring loss. In fact no fishnet unit in the study area has incurred a loss in the last 10 years. But the negative growth shows that in terms of gross profit there is a declining trend over the succeeding years. Hence, they have shown a negative growth. The negative growth is represented as no growth in the study. The negative growth rate of gross profit went upto 25 per cent in different fishnet units in Kanyakumari district. Even among the units showing positive growth, the result is not significant. It is clear that 46 per cent of the units (40 units) have reached a meager growth up to 10 per cent in the last 10 years, which is not a significant one.

Analysis of growth of gross profit in fishnet units gives the conclusion that in Kanyakumari district in terms of gross profit fishnet units have not grown well. The main reason for this state in fishnet industry in Kanyakumari District is that though sales is increasing over the years, increase in competition among the fishnet units pressurises them competitively to reduce their selling prices. It results in reduction of gross profit over the years. Hence the number of fishnet units earned huge gross profit has come down in recent years. It is the main reason for the non growth of fishnet units in terms of gross profit.

NET PROFIT

Net profit is often referred to as the bottom line. Net profit is calculated by subtracting a company's total expenses from total revenue. Net profit shows what the company has earned or lost in a given period of time (usually one year). It is also called as net income or net earnings.

The Net profit margin is indicative of management's ability to operate the business with sufficient success. Net profit recovers the cost of merchandise or service, the expense of operating the business (including depreciation) and the cost of the borrowed funds from gross profit. Net profit also leaves a margin of reasonable compensation to the owners for providing their capital at risk. The ratio of net profit (after interest and tax) in sales expresses the cost price effectiveness of the operation[6].

A higher net profit ensures adequate return to the owners. It also enables a firm to withstand against adverse economic conditions. When selling price is declining, cost of production is rising and demand for the product is falling the net profit comes down. A low net profit has the opposite implications[7].

Fishnet units in Kanyakumari district have been earning reasonable net profit over years. While in the initial years net profit was high, in course of time, due to the increase in the financial and administrative expenses this has declined. Fluctuating Net Profit among fishnet units over the last 10 years ending with 2008 indicates the instability in fishnet industry. Compound Growth Rate calculated comprehends the differing net profit among fishnet units in the last 10 years into a single year. Growth of net profit among fishnet units in Kanyakumari District is presented in Table 3.2.

Table 3.2: Growth of Fishnet Units in Terms of Net profit

Sl. No.	Growth (in Percentage)	Number of Units	Percentage
1.	(-) 25-0	55	63.22
2.	0-5	27	31.03
3.	5-10	4	4.60
4.	Above 10	1	1.15
	Total	**87**	**100.00**

Source: Primary data

It is observed from the present study that a majority of the fishnet manufacturing units (63.22%) in Kanyakumari district have not achieved growth in terms of net profit in the last 10 years ending year 2008. Hence their CGR (Compound Growth Rate) is negative or less than zero. These units are represented as non growth units. The net profit of non growth concerns ranging from 0 to -25 per cent. It is important to note that in most of the cases the growth was only up to zero per cent in the last 10 years. It is further clear that only 36.78 per cent of the fishnet units have shown a positive growth in terms of net profit. The growth of such concerns in the last 10 years, ranged between 0 to 15 per cent. Even among the units showing positive growth, many of the units (31.03%) have shown a meagre growth which was up to 5 per cent only.

The reason attributed for negative growth in terms of net profit is that the increasing administrative and financial cost of the firms in the last 10 years decreased the net profit considerably. To meet their financial requirements, firms go for borrowed sources, which became a burden to them. Over dependence on borrowed fund ultimately resulted in increase in financial cost and thereby yielding low net profit.

A comparative analysis of the growth rates of gross profit and net profit in the last 10 years in fishnet industry in Kanyakumari district shows a close synchronisation among them. Both of them show that most of the units manufacturing fishnet have been negative in terms of profit. It is clear that the cost of production of fishnet units is on increase over the past 10 years, which is a burden to fishnet units in Kanyakumari district.

PRODUCTION CAPACITY

Production capacity represents the volume of finished products that can be produced by an industrial unit or plant or industry as the maximum in a given period of time by using normal resources. Production capacity of an industrial unit in the same industry varies from unit to unit which primarily depends upon availability of machines, quality of raw-materials used availability of power, manpower and the like. It also depends upon the availability of power and electricity and water. Many other similar factors determine the production capacity of an industrial unit. In fishnet units, production of fishnet and nylon yarn depends mainly upon the type of machinery used. Machines imported from abroad are capable of producing more volume than the machines made in inland. The cost of foreign machinery is much higher than the machine made in India. Hence, depending upon the financial availability either foreign machinery or inland machinery is installed in fishnet units. However, both the types of machines are equally used in fishnet units in Kanyakumari district. Many of the fishnet units which have started with single machinery have added two and more machines over time. Hence, in course of time, the production capacity of the fishnet have grown manifold. The details of growth of production capacity of the fishnet units in Kanyakumari district is presented in Table 3.3.

Table 3.3: Growth of Fishnet Units in Terms of Production Capacity

Sl. No.	Growth (in Percentage)	Number of Units	Percentage
1.	(-) 5-0	37	42.53
2.	0-5	50	57.47
	Total	**87**	**100.00**

Source: Primary data.

Table 3.3 shows that the production capacity of the fishnet units in the study area has grown in the past 10 years. It is clear that 57.47 per cent of fishnet units have shown positive growth ranging between 0 to 5 per cent. However, the fishnet units with a negative growth rate are also high in Kanyakumari district. It is found that 42.53 per cent of the total fishnet units studied has recorded negative growth which ranges between 0 and -5 per cent. The negative growth implies dropping of existing machines. Fishnet units have dropped their existing machinery either because of obsolescence or mechanical failure. It also implies that in the recent years new machineries have not been added for production due to low demand arising from heavy competition in the market.

SALES

Sales is otherwise represented as turnover. It is the final activity of any enterprise towards which all other activities are focused on. Increase in the volume of sales is an act of completion of a commercial activity. Sales is an important indicator of growth of any business unit. Further, sales is the key determinant of profit. Those units which are positive in their industrial activity alone are able to increase their sales. Similarly, only if the industrial unit has a very positive environment in all respects, it will show growth in terms of sales. Though every industrial unit is trying its best to increase its sales from its current level, only a few could succeed. In fishnet industry those units which produce high quality products have a good command in the market. All other units which lack in quality lack behind these units. The growth recorded by fishnet units in the last 10 years in terms of sales in Kanyakumari district is presented in Table 3.4.

Table 3.4: Growth of Fishnet Units in Terms of Sales

Sl. No.	Growth (in Percentage)	Number of units	Percentage
1.	(-) 5-0	7	8.05
2.	0-5	34	39.08
3.	5-10	40	45.97
4.	10-15	4	4.60
5.	15-20	2	2.30
	Total	**87**	**100.00**

Source: Primary data.

It is very significant to note from the Table 3.4 that the sales volume has grown well in fishnet units in Kanyakumari district in the last 10 years. It is interesting to find that growth of most of the fishnet units have shown a positive growth in terms of sales. It can be seen from the table that 85 per cent of the fishnet units have shown a positive growth that ranges from 0 per cent to 10 per cent in the last 10 years. A very minimum number of fishnet units (6 out of 87 units) have a significant growth ranging from 10 per cent to 20 per cent. Similarly, hardly 7 fishnet units (8%) alone have made a negative growth in terms of Compound Growth Rate with regard to sales.

Analysis of the data reveals that in terms of sales, fishnet units have grown well in Kanyakumari district. Hence most of the fishnet units have shown a better growth. The main reason for the increase in sales volume in the past 10 years is that the demand for fishnet is growing steadily due to mechanisation of fishing crafts and expansion of local market to state level. Further, the demand for fishnet is growing well at the national level. Similarly, a few industrial units have expanded their market horizons to the international level. All these factors have resulted in growth of sales in fishnet units.

CAPACITY UTILISED

Capacity utilisation refers to the extent to which an enterprise actually uses its installed productive capacity. It refers to the relationship between actual output that is produced with the installed equipments and the potential output which could be produced with it[8]. Utilisation of installed capacity depends upon many factors like demand, potential marketing ability and availability of resources like raw material. Fishnet units which are able to market their product effectively utilise their capacity to the fullest extent, while the others who are lacking behind in marketing under utilise their capacity. Similarly, other factors cited above are responsible for under utilisation of capacity. The details of capacity utilisation by fishnet units in Kanyakumari district is furnished in Table 3.5.

Table 3.5: Growth of Fishnet Units in Terms of Capacity Utilisation

Sl. No.	Growth (in Percentage)	Number of units	Percentage
1.	(-) 5-0	2	2.30
2.	0-5	38	43.68
3.	5-10	45	51.72
4.	Above 10	2	2.30
	Total	**87**	**100.00**

Source: Primary data.

An observation on the capacity utilisation of the fishnet units in the study area through Table 3.5 shows that 85 fishnet units (97.70%) out of 87 fishnet units have shown positive growth in terms of capacity utilisation. The Compound Growth Rate of capacity utilisation in such cases ranges between zero and 20 per cent. It is a significant growth. In case of 43.68 per cent of the fishnet units, the rate of growth is between 0 and 5 per cent. In majority of the cases (51.72% fishnet units) the rate of growth ranged from 5 per cent to 10 per cent. It is very significant to note that fishnet manufacturing units showing negative Compound Growth Rate in terms of capacity utilisation is very meagre in number (only 2 fishnet units out of 87 fishnet units studied) in Kanyakumari district.

The increase in capacity utilisation clearly shows the increase in production. Uninterrupted supply of raw materials and expansion of market area are the major reasons attributable for the growth of capacity utilisation in the fishnet industry in Kanyakumari district.

Capital Employed

Capital employed is an indicator of growth of an industrial unit. Capital employed represents the financial commitment of the entrepreneur in the enterprise. It also represents the assets held by the entrepreneur in the enterprise. Capital employed can be represented in many ways.

Capital employed is usually represented as total asset less current liabilities or non-current assets plus working capital. Otherwise, capital employed can be defined as equity plus loan which are subject to interest. Otherwise, capital employed represents total assets less non interest bearing liabilities. From the foregoing analysis of capital employed, it can be concluded that capital employed represents the following:

(i) The total amount of capital used for the acquisition of profits

(ii) The value of all the assets employed in a business.

(iii) Fixed assets plus working capital.

(iv) Total assets less current liabilities.

In fishnet units the entrepreneur either invests his/her own money or borrowed money from friends, banks and financial institutions. This becomes the capital of the enterprise. Similarly, the capital employed is locked up in the land, buildings, machineries, fittings and furnitures and many other assets. Growth of capital employed over years indicates the growth of the industrial unit.

Table 3.6 furnishes the growth of capital employed in fishnet industry in Kanyakumari district.

Table 3.6: Growth of Fishnet Units in Terms of Capital Employed

Sl. No.	Growth (in Percentage)	Number of units	Percentage
1.	(-) 10 - (-) 5	12	13.79
2.	(-) 5-0	41	47.13
3.	0-5	9	10.34
4.	5-10	10	11.49
5.	10-15	13	14.95
6.	Above 15	2	2.30
	Total	**87**	**100.00**

Source: Primary data.

Table 3.6 reveals that most of the fishnet manufacturing units in Kanyakumari district have shown a negative growth in terms of capital employed. In case of 47.13 per cent of the fishnet units functioning in

Kanyakumari district, the rate of growth in terms of capital employed ranges between zero to (-) 5 per cent and in case of another 13.79 per cent of the fishnet units, the growth went to (-) 5 to (-) 10 per cent. Only 39.08 per cent of the fishnet units had a positive growth in terms of capital employed in the last 10 years. The rate in the above cases varies between zero per cent to 25 per cent. However, the rate of growth in most of the cases was limited to 15 per cent. Fifteen per cent growth in capital employed in 10 years span is not a remarkable growth to any industry.

The negative growth in terms of capital employed in fishnet units implies non introduction of additional capital by the owners. It further reveals that entrepreneurs are not so interested in developing the fishnet units by infusing additional funds. Instead, they would have withdrawn money from their business which would resulting in a negative growth in capital employed.

EMPLOYEES

Employee represents the manpower employed in an enterprise. An employee contributes his/her labour and expertise to an endeavor for remuneration. Employees perform the discrete activity of economic production with the support of the other three factors of production namely land, capital and organisation. An employee is hired by an employer to do a specific job. Labour is the important factor, based on which the entire production operation of the industrial unit depends. The size of the employment generated by an industrial unit is a good indicator measuring the growth of the unit.

To meet the commercial demand for the product in the market production is increased. Increase in production is attained only through addition of employees. When business grows positively, increase in the number of employees is quite inevitable. Employees may be skilled, unskilled, semi-skilled or administrative staff. Skilled employee represents the workers with specific talents. A few specific category of work can be done only by employees with specific talents. Such workers are represented as skilled workers. On the contrary to carry a few jobs no specific technical talents are demanded from the employees. Anyone without any specific technical talents could do such job. Such workers require no specific talents. They are referred to as unskilled workers. Semi-skilled workers are those who are partially talented with specific skills. Other than these, there are administrative staff who engage in official work or executive work. Remuneration payable to each of these different categories of labour is different. Increase in the number of employees of different categories over years indicates the growth of the industrial unit.

In fishnet units, operators who are directly engaged in producing fishnet or nylon yarn are skilled workers. Semi-skilled workers support the skilled workers in their job. Unskilled workers carry manual works like mending the fishnet, packaging and other works which are related to the fishnet manufacturing. Unskilled workers facilitate smooth production without interruption. Beyond this, another way to look on employees is on the basis of permanency in job. In this classification, there are permanent employees, temporary employees, and part-time employees. Permanent employees are permanent in nature. They are subject to several labour laws like Factories Act, Employee State Insurance (ESI) Act, Provident Fund (PF) Act, Workmen's Compensation Act, and the like. All other categories of employees are not permanent.

Similarly, men and women are equally employed in different jobs in fishnet industry. However, women cannot be employed in night shift because of the compulsion of law. Table 3.7 outlines the growth of fishnet industry in Kanyakumari district in terms of employment.

Table 3.7: Growth of Fishnet Industry in Terms of Employees

Sl. No.	Growth (in Percentage)	Number of units	Percentage
1.	(-) 15 – (-) 10	1	1.15
2.	(-) 10 – (-) 5	10	11.49
3.	(-) 5 – 0	33	37.94
4.	0 – 5	18	20.69
5.	5 – 10	15	17.24
6.	10 – 15	9	10.34
7.	Above 15	1	1.15
	Total	**87**	**100.00**

Source: Primary data.

Analysis of Compound Growth Rate with respect to number of persons employed in fishnet manufacturing units through Table 3.7 reveals the fact that more than half of the fishnet units studied (that is 50.58%) have achieved only a negative growth. Only 49.42 per cent of the fishnet units studied have showed a positive growth in terms of employment generation. But the rate of growth in such units is very meager. Out of the 87 fishnet units studied, only one fishnet unit has registered a growth above 15 per cent. It shows that fishnet units in Kanyakumari district have not recorded growth in terms of employment generation.

The high incidence of labour turnover is identified to be the reason for the slow growth of fishnet units in Kanyakumari district in terms of employees. The high labour turnover in this industry arises mainly due to quitting of job by women employees. In many of the fishnet units in Kanyakumari district, most of the employees are women who quit their work once they get married. Another major segment of employees quit their job in order to join other jobs with higher pay. Hence, labour turnover is always a problem in fishnet industry in Kanyakumari district.

Absence of transport facilities to bring women workers from their residence to the industrial place also motivates the women workers to resign their job. Absence of good remuneration package and other facilities could have been another reason promoting the employees to resign their job. However, the turnover of workers did not affect production capacity and volume of production as evidenced through analysis in Table 3.3, and 3.5. Then, the reason might be that the shortage of work force is compensated in the sector by over time employment of the existing workforce. So regular production needed to meet the demand is not affected. Thus, it is hard to conclude that the lower growth in terms of employees indicates lower growth in fishnet industry in Kanyakumari district.

ASSETS OWNED

Resources with economic value that an individual or corporation owns or controls with the expectation that it will provide future benefits are known as assets. In the context of accounting, assets are classified into current assets and fixed (non-current) assets. Current assets are those assets which are liquid in nature. The assets which could be converted into cash in short term without much difficulty are referred to as current assets. Current assets include cash, accounts receivables and inventory. Fixed assets are those that are kept for providing benefits for more than one year. Fixed assets help the firm to increase their profit earning capacity. It is more or less permanent in nature. Fixed assets include machinery, building and land.

The value of assets owned by an industrial unit indicates the financial solvency. Growth of assets is an indicator of growth of the business unit. The total value of assets of the fishnet units varies from fishnet unit to fishnet unit. Further, over the last 10 years the value of assets (both current and non current assets) has been fluctuating among most of the fishnet units in Kanyakumari district. The table 3.8 shows the growth of fishnet units in terms of assets owned.

It is observed from the Table 3.8 that 57.47 per cent of the total fishnet units surveyed in the study have shown positive growth in terms of asset value in the past 10 years. Further, it is found in the study that 57.47 per cent (50 fishnet units out of total 87 units) have registered a growth ranging up to 15 per cent, whereas, in case of 35.63 per cent of the fishnet units, it is up to 5 per cent only. The growth in terms of asset value increase is due to increase

Table 3.8: Growth of Fishnet Industry in Terms of Assets Owned

Sl. No.	Growth (in Percentage)	Number of Units	Percentage
1.	(-) 10 - (-) 5	2	2.30
2.	(-) 5 - 0	35	40.23
3.	0 - 5	31	35.63
4.	5 - 10	16	18.39
5.	10 - 15	3	3.45
	Total	**87**	**100.00**

Source: Primary data.

in the land value. In recent years real assets including land have appreciated manifold. In Kanyakumari district also the similar tendency of growth has happened. As the outcome, values of assets of the fishnet units in Kanyakumari district have considerably appreciated. But, in case of 40.23 per cent of the units surveyed in the study, the growth in terms of the assets value has gone down up to (-) 5 per cent in the last 10 years. In case of another 2.30 per cent of the fishnet units, the negative growth has ranged between (-) 5 per cent to (-) 10 per cent. Such a negative growth was witnessed in fishnet industry in Kanyakumari district as the outcome of major repairs and obsolescence in machinery. Many fishnet units have condemned their out dated machineries in the recent past. Another reason for the reduction in value of the asset is that, due to continuous usage, the value of building and machinery depreciated considerably. All of these factors made a reduction in the value of assets held by fishnet units.

EXTERNAL LIABILITIES

External liabilities are the liabilities of the industrial unit which are due to outside parties. Since the owner himself/herself can not contribute the entire amount needed for the industrial units, he/she borrow money from external parties. External borrowings are inevitable. Fishnet units borrow money from outside parties such as friends, relatives, banks and financial institutions for their financial needs. This amount due to outside parties constitutes the external liability. A growing firm shall wipe out such external liabilities in course of time. Those units which reduce external liabilities achieve growth while the others who could not reduce the external liabilities fall down in their growth or grow slowly. Table 3.9 shows the growth recorded by fishnet units in Kanyakumari district as evidenced in external liabilities.

Table 3.9: Growth of Fishnet Units in Terms of External Liabilities

Sl. No.	Growth (in Percentage)	Number of units	Percentage
1.	(-) 20 - (-) 15	9	10.34
2.	(-) 15 - (-) 10	7	8.05
3.	(-) 10 - (-) 5	20	22.99
4.	(-) 5 - 0	28	32.18
5.	0 - 5	7	8.05
6.	5 - 10	9	10.34
7.	10 - 15	6	6.90
8.	15 - 20	1	1.15
	Total	**87**	**100.00**

Source: Primary data.

It is significant to note that in most of the cases (73.56%) in the study area the growth of fishnet units in terms of external liabilities is negative. The negative growth is ranging from zero per cent to (-) 20 per cent. Further, it can be seen that in majority of the cases, the negative growth has gone upto (-) 10 per cent. Only 26.44 per cent of the fishnet units in Kanyakumari district have achieved a positive growth which is ranging up to 20 per cent in the last 10 year period. The fishnet units with high positive growth (15% to 20%) are meager in number (1 out of 87 fishnet units). Hence, it shows that fishnet units in Kanyakumari have not grown well in terms of external liabilities.

The lower growth or negative/no growth recorded by fishnet units in terms of external liabilities is due to lack of adequate supply of finance from external sources like bank and government agencies like TIIC (Tamilnadu Industrial Investment Corporation).

RAW MATERIALS UTILISED

Raw materials are the unfinished products purchased for further processing. It is the input for the production process. The raw materials purchased for production are converted into finished product by the production process. Major production cost incurred by any industrial unit is on the purchase of raw materials. Any deficiency in the quality of the raw materials affects the quality of the finished product. Inefficient purchase and inefficient utilisation of raw materials result in increased production cost with sub-standard finished product.

In the growth process, an industrial unit showing growth spends more on raw material year after year. Because of the usage of high quality raw materials and increase in purchase rate, the purchase cost of raw materials of the industrial unit increases over years. Further, due to increase in production every unit consumes more volumes of raw material. So to achieve growth, an industrial unit consumes more raw materials and spends much on raw materials. Hence, growth in purchase of raw materials is an indicator of growth of the industrial unit. Fishnet units in Kanyakumari district have grown by consuming more volume of raw- materials. Table 3.10 shows the details of utilisation of raw materials by fishnet units in Kanyakumari district.

Table 3.10: Growth of Fishnet Units in Terms of Raw Materials Utilised

Sl. No.	Growth (in Percentage)	Number of Units	Percentage
1.	(-) 20 - (-) 15	3	3.45
2.	(-) 15 - (-) 10	2	2.30
3.	(-) 10 - (-) 5	0	0.00
4.	(-) 5 - 0	12	13.79
5.	0 - 5	14	16.09
6.	5 - 10	25	28.74
7.	10 - 15	18	20.69
8.	15 - 20	2	2.30
9.	20 - 25	11	12.64
	Total	**87**	**100.00**

Source: Primary data.

It is observed from the study that raw materials utilisation in most of the fishnet units (70 out of 87 fishnet units) showed a positive growth in the last 10 years. Among the growth units, the growth was high and went up to 25 per cent. Another 19.54 per cent of the fishnet units in Kanyakumari district have a negative growth which was up to (-) 20 per cent.

The higher number of fishnet units with positive growth implies the fact that fishnet units in Kanyakumari district have achieved a significant growth in the past 10 years in terms of raw materials used. Such a growth in terms of raw material utilisation endorses the growth in terms of production and capacity utilisation which is already analysed in Table 3.3.

MEASUREMENT OF GROWTH

Though the growth of fishnet units have been measured individually with respect to 10 components, overall growth could not be ascertained concretely. There is no readymade measure available to generalise the level of growth achieved by fishnet units in definite terms. Therefore, employing scaling method becomes inevitable to the researcher to measure the overall growth of fishnet units in Kanyakumari district. Growth scale has been constructed with the 10 components with which individual growth has been ascertained. A growth scale with a maximum of (+) 100 scores and a minimum of (-) 100 scores was constructed for analysis. The scores were distributed among the ten variables (components) equally at the rate of (+) or (-) 10 scores for each component. For each 10 per cent growth a score of (+)1 or (-)1 is assigned. Since all the ten components are of equal nature, invariably equal weightage is assigned to each component. Each component was assigned (+) or (-) 10 scores. Table 3.11 shows the growth scale and scores allotted for 10 variables (components) identified for measuring the growth.

Table 3.11: Growth Scale with Individual Component Scores

Sl. No.	Growth Components	Score Range	
		For Growth Units	For Non-growth Units
1.	Gross profit	0 - (+) 10	0 - (-)10
2.	Net profit	0 - (+) 10	0 - (-) 10
3.	Production capacity	0 - (+) 10	0 - (-) 10
4.	Sales	0 - (+) 10	0 - (-) 10
5.	Capacity utilised	0 - (+) 10	0 - (-) 10
6.	Capital Employed	0 - (+) 10	0 - (-) 10
7.	Employee	0 - (+) 10	0 - (-) 10
8.	Asset owned	0 - (+) 10	0 - (-) 10
9.	External Liabilities	0 - (+) 10	0 - (-) 10
10.	Raw material utilised	0 - (+) 10	0 - (-) 10
	Total	**0 - (+) 100**	**0 - (-) 100**

Source: Primary data.

As shown in Table 3.11, the maximum scores allotted for positive growth is (+) 100 and the minimum scores allotted for negative growth is (-) 100. Each one of the ten variables (components) is given invariably (+) or (-) 10 scores. The distribution of scores for each variable depends upon the CGR (Compound Growth Rate) achieved by each fishnet unit in the last 10 years. The details of scores awarded for different variables are furnished in Table 3.12.

Table 3.12: Scores Allotted for Each Variable in Growth Scale

Sl. No.	Growth Rate (CGR) Percentage	Scores	
		If Growth is Positive	If Growth is Negative
1.	(+)/(-) 0 to 10	1	-1
2.	(+)/(-) 10 to 20	2	-2
3.	(+)/(-) 20 to 30	3	-3
4.	(+)/(-) 30 to 40	4	-4
5.	(+)/(-) 40 to 50	5	-5
6.	(+)/(-) 50 to 60	6	-6
7.	(+)/(-) 60 to 70	7	-7
8.	(+)/(-) 70 to 80	8	-8
9.	(+)/(-) 80 to 90	9	-9
10.	(+)/(-) 90 to 100	10	-10

Source: Primary data.

Table 3.12 exhibits the scores allotted for each of the 10 components for different levels of growth in terms of CGR (Compound Growth Rate) attained by different fishnet units in the last 10 years. Those units which do not show any growth or negative growth (CGR) are awarded 'zero' scores or negative score. Because of this reason, they are called as non-growth units. On the contrary, the firms which have shown positive growth (CGR) in respect of each of the 10 components of the growth scale are awarded scores progressively as they show higher growth rate.

GROWTH OF FISHNET UNITS

In order to have an overview of the variation in growth, a component wise analysis has been attempted. Scores have been allotted to each of the fishnet unit for the 10 components as shown in Table 3.13. Component-wise growth analysis is useful to identify the most important component. This has the significant role in the overall growth of the fishnet units. Table 3.13 shows the component-wise growth of fishnet units in Kanyakumari district.

It is evident from Table 3.13 that individually growth score is the highest in respect of the components net profit, production capacity and capacity utilisation. Each of the components have obtained 87 scores out of the maximum 870 scores, with means score 6.85 representing 10 per cent of the maximum scores. The sales is the next component standing in the second position, with the total score of 73 out of 870 scores with means score 0.83 representing 8.39 percentage of the maximum scores. The component raw material utilised stands in the third position with a score of 70 (mean score 0.80) representing 8.05 per cent of the maximum scores. The components ranking fourth place, are employee and assets owned. Each of them had the score of 47. All the other components have obtained very low scores. They are gross profit (4.6 per cent) with 0.46 mean score, capital Employed (4.25 per cent) with 0.42 mean score, and assets owned (2.76 per cent) with 0.28 mean score. The analysis shows that the components net profit, production capacity and capacity utilisation have significant role in the overall growth of fishnet units in Kanyakumari district.

Table 3.13: Component-wise Growth of Fishnet Units in Kanyakumari District

Sl. No.	Growth Components	Scores Awarded		Maximum Score (87 x 10=870)	Percentage of Maximum score
		Total	Mean Score		
1.	Gross profit	40	0.46	870	4.60
2.	Net profit	87	1.00	870	10.00
3.	Production Capacity	87	1.00	870	10.00
4.	Sales	73	0.83	870	8.39
5.	Capacity utilised	87	1.00	870	10.00
6.	Capital Employed	37	0.42	870	4.25
7.	Employee	47	0.53	870	5.40
8.	Assets owned	47	0.53	870	5.40
9.	External Liabilities	24	0.28	870	2.76
10.	Raw material utilised	70	0.80	870	8.05
	Total	**599**	**6.85**	**8700**	**68.85**

Source: Primary data.

STATE OF GROWTH

Each of the respondent units covered in the study have differing growth. While a group of units have recorded growth in respect of all the ten components, another group of fishnet units have recorded negative growth or no growth. Another set of fishnet units have positive growth in respect of a few variables while negative growth in respect of other variables. Similarly, different units have different growth. The extent of growth of the fishnet units in the past 10 years as evidenced through different components with respect to 87 fishnet units functioning in Kanyakumari district is presented in this part. The growth scale comprises of 10 components each carrying 10 scores on either side (Positive, Negative) measures the growth. The positive growth (Calculated through CGR) implies that fishnet units have grown positively in the last 10 years while the negative growth implies that fishnet units have grown negatively in the last 10 years. Thus, the maximum score one respondent unit can obtain is (+) 100 and the minimum score one respondent can obtain is (-) 100. All the respondent units have scores ranging between (-) 100 to (+) 100.

It is interesting to find that the growth scores obtained by 87 fishnet units ranged between (-) 5 to (+) 20. No fishnet unit in Kanyakumari district had either the score above (+) 20 or below (-) 5. The details of the growth scores of the respondent units are presented in Table 3.14.

Table 3.14 Growth Scores of Fishnet Units

Sl. No.	Growth Scores	No. of units	Percentage
1.	(-) 5 - 0	8	9.20
2.	0 - 5	28	32.18
3.	5 - 10	37	42.53
4.	10 - 15	9	10.34
5.	15 - 20	5	5.75
	Total	**87**	**100.00**

Source: Primary data.

It is clear from the Table 3.14 that 74.71 per cent of the fishnet units in Kanyakumari district have the growth with scores ranging between 0 to 10. The other units have shown an in significant growth. Hence, it is concluded that the extent of growth of fishnet units is very low.

In order to evaluate the state of growth arithmetic mean has been calculated from the total scores obtained by all the 87 respondents. The total of arithmetic mean is 6.05. Taking arithmetic mean as the base fishnet units in Kanyakumari district are classified into two groups.

Fishnet units which scored below 6.05 are put under the group that has achieved negative growth/no growth. Fishnet units that scored above 6.05 are placed in the second group that has achieved growth. Table 3.15 shows the classification of the total fishnet units in Kanyakumari district into two growth groups viz., non growth units and growth units.

It is seen from Table 3.15 that 51 fishnet units (58.62%) in Kanyakumari district have achieved negative growth (non growth). The other 36 fishnet units in the study area are regarded as growth units in Kanyakumari district of the reason that their growth has been above the mean (6.05) score. The reason behind this non-growth units is that fishnet units in this group have suffered much with respect to capital, external liabilities and gross profit. This is the reason why more number of fishnet units have fallen under the category of non-growth in the last 10 years in fishnet industry in Kanyakumari district.

Table 3.15: State of Growth of Fishnet Units in Kanyakumari District

Sl. No	State of Growth	No. of Respondents	Percentage
1.	Non-Growth Units	51	58.62
2.	Growth Units	36	41.38
	Total	87	**100.00**

Source: Primary data.

DIMENSIONS OF GROWTH — MULTIPLE DISCRIMINANT ANALYSIS

Multivariate analysis seeks to predict industrial growth using a methodology that considers the combined influence of several variables. The multivariable technique, commonly used in predicting business growth or non-growth, is Multiple Discriminant Analysis.

Multiple discriminant technique helps in classifying the observation into one of the several pre-specific groups on the basis of certain characteristics of the observation. It involves estimating a mathematical function which discriminates the best between the groups. Discriminant Analysis has been widely used for the identification of the growth / no growth industrial units and also for the prediction of growth[9].

Edward Altman, W.H. Beaver Edward Dedkins, Tafler, Delton Chesser, C.D. Bhattacharya, K.B. Mehta. R.A, Yadave S.S. Srivastava Murti, Mark Blum, Mayor and Pilfer have made useful contributions in the field. The important common features of all of these studies are:

Groups: Classification of the units into two groups namely growth units and Non- growth units.

Dependent Variables: Industrial growth.

Discriminant Variable: Financial ratios.

Assumption: Financial ratios used for dicriminant analysis satisfy the condition of normal distribution.

Methodology of Discriminant Analysis

Discriminant analysis involves an elaborate analysis process which includes:

- **Determination of classification group**

  First, on some reasonable basis of observation, groups are classified. There can be two or more groups. Classification is done as per the specific requirement of the research problem.

- **Selection of the predictor Variables**

  A comprehensive list of predictor variables useful for the enquiry is drawn. Out of this list, the variables considered relevant and useful for the purpose of discrimination are selected. These variables are interval scaled. Different combination of variables considered to be most useful for the purpose of discrimination is selected. The variables finally selected represent the characteristic features of all the different groups.

- **Sample from each group**

  A separate sample is taken from each group. In the process of selection of samples, first the universe is clearly defined, and identified. Then, a sample of adequate size is selected from each group by random sampling method.

- **Collection of data**

  Basic data required for discriminant analysis is collected either from secondary source or through a primary survey. The questionnaire is designed to cover all predictor variables comprehensively.

- **Data Analysis**

  Once the data matrix is ready, step by step analysis is made through determination of mean of each variable for each group. Then their difference in the determination of standard deviation and their differences for each group, inverse of the dispersion matrix, co-efficient of linear discriminant function, relative importance of variables and cut-off point are calculated.

- **Confusion Matrix .**

  A confusion matrix is drawn to compare the actual classification of items on the basis of discriminant function.

- **Mis-classification probability**

  It is determined to find out the probability of an individual case belonging to group I, being classified as belonging to group II. This indicates inadequate ability of the linear discriminant function to classify correctly[10].

Edward Altman is the first person to successfully use, step wise Multiple Discriminant Analysis to develop a prediction model with high degree of accuracy. He used a sample of 66 companies, of which 33 failed and 33 successful. Altman's model is a measurement of the financial health of a company and a powerful tool to diagnose the profitability of a company that will go insolvent within a 27 years period. Altman's model achieved an accuracy rate of 95 per cent.

The 'Z' score (Bankruptcy- predictor variable) combines several of the most significant variables in a statistically derived combination. The 'Z' score bankruptcy predictor combines five common business ratios. The model was originally developed on a sampling of manufacturing firms. However, the algorithm he has developed consistently reported to have 95 per cent accuracy. Later, there have been many other bankruptcy predictors developed and published. However, none has been so thoroughly tested and broadly accepted as the Altman's 'Z' score.

Subsequently, Edward Altman developed another model by examining 85 manufacturing companies in the year 1968. He developed 'Z' scores for private manufacturing companies (Z score - model *A*) and another for general/ service firms (Z score- Model *B*)[11].

Subsequent to Edward Altman, several other personalities devised several other models. The models developed in later years had drawbacks. Hence, they could not succeed. Further, each of the model so discussed have limited applicability to specified areas. Hence, no generalisation could be drawn.

In the present study C.D. Bhattacharya model is applied. Because, Bhattacharya has applied Multiple Discriminant Analysis in a similar situation very similar to the one in which the present study is attempted.

The model used by Prof. C.D. Bhattacharya is slightly modified by the researcher to study the growth of fishnet industry in Kanyakumari district. Since the predictor variables used by the researcher have been validated in the C.D. Bhattacharya model, no validation of the test is attempted in the study.

The discriminant value (Z) calculated through discriminant functions in the study is written as.

$Z = b_1x_1 + b_2x_2 + b_3x_3 + b_4x_4 + b_5x_5$

Where Z = Discriminant value of an industrial unit

b_1, b_2, b_3, b_4, b_5 = Discriminant coefficients

x_1, x_2, x_3, x_4, x_5 = Predictor variables

x_1 = Working capital to Total Asset

x_2 = Return on capital employed

x_3 = Gross profit/loss to Total Asset

x_4 = Net worth to Total Liabilities

x_5 = Sales to Total Assets

Growth is a continuing state of affair which is not limited to any particular year. Hence, predictor variables namely the ratios named x_1, x_2, x_3, x_4, x_5 have been calculated for each fishnet unit by taking average figures for the last 10 years ending with 2007-08. In multiple disciminant analysis, grouping of fishnet units is to be done on some basis.

In the present study, in the component-wise analysis of growth, fishnet units in Kanyakumari district have been grouped into two categories namely, Growth units and Non-Growth units (the details are presented in the first part of the chapter). The same categorisation is employed in this part for Multiple Discriminant Analysis. Multiple Discriminant Analysis is attempted through SPSS.

The discriminant function formed in analysis is:

$$Z = -0.059x_1 + 0.434x_2 - 0.490x_3 + 0.264x_4 + 0.537x_5$$

Using this discriminant function, 'Z' score for all fishnet units in Kanyakumari district have been calculated. On the basis of the 'Z' scores calculated, fishnet units in Kanyakumari district are classified. The details of classification are presented in Table 3.16.

Table 3.16: Fishnet Units with Different 'Z' Scores

Sl. No.	Z Scores	Number of Units	Percentage
1.	Below 0	23	26.44
2.	0 - 20	23	26.44
3.	20 - 40	20	22.98
4.	40 - 60	7	8.05
5.	60 - 80	9	10.34
6.	80 - 100	2	2.30
7.	Above 100	3	3.45
	Total	**87**	**100.00**

Source: Primary data.

As it is evident from Table 3.16 that 26.44 per cent of the total fishnet units in Kanyakumari district had the 'Z' score below zero. Similarly, 16.09

per cent of the fishnet units had the 'Z' score above 60. Hence, it can be concluded that most of the fishnet units in Kanyakumari district had the 'Z' scores ranging upto 40 in the past 10 years.

In order to find out the prediction efficiency of the Multiple Discriminent Analysis with respect to 'Z' scores, a confusion matrix is drawn and is presented in Table 3.17.

Table 3.17: Confusion Matrix

Category	Predicted Group Membership		Total
	Non Growth Units	Growth Units	
Original count			
Non growth units	36.00	15.00	51
Growth units	16.00	20.00	36
Percentage			
Non growth units	70.59	29.41	100
Growth units	44.44	55.56	100

Prediction efficiency is 64.4 per cent.

Source: Primary data.

The Table 3.17 shows that the Multiple Discriminant Analysis conducted in the study has the prediction efficiency of 64.4 per cent. It is because, out of 51 fishnet units observed as the non-growth units, 15 fishnet units have fallen under the second group i.e. growth group. Similarly, out of 36 fishnet units observed as growth units 16 have fallen under the non-growth units. However, Multiple Discriminant Analysis attempted in the study had reliable prediction efficiency of 64.4 per cent. The prediction efficiency of the Multiple Discriminant Analysis approves the observed classification of fishnet units through scaling technique as correct. Hence, it can be concluded that fishnet units is Kanyakumari district have not grown well.

SUMMARY

In this chapter the growth of fishnet industry in Kanyakumari district has been analysed. Ten components have been identified as components for the analysis of growth. They are Gross profit, Net profit, Production capacity, Sales, Capacity utilised, Capital employed, Number of employees, Assets owned, External liabilities and Raw materials utilised. In order to compute the extent of growth, a growth scale has been constructed with the above 10 components. With the help of the scale, growth scores have been awarded to all the 87 respondent fishnet units. The total scores obtained by fishnet units for each component in the growth scale is given in this chapter. Based on the individual scores obtained, all the respondent fishnet units are classified into two groups namely growth units and non growth units. The study identified 36 fishnet units as growth units and 51 as non growth units. It shows that majority of the fishnet units are non growth units in Kanyakumari district. Further, the Multiple Discriminant Analysis is applied to find out the 'Z' score of growth for fishnet units. The confusion matrix worked out in Multiple Discriminant Analysis showed a high prediction efficiency (64.4%), which approves the observed classification made through growth scale. Hence, the study concludes that the growth of fishnet units in Kanyakumari district is not remarkable.

REFERENCES

1. Khanka, S.S., *Entrepreneurial Development*, S. Chand & Company Limited, New Delhi, 2008, pp. 313-314.
2. Churchill, N.C., Lewis, V.L., *The Stages of Small Business Growth*, Harvard Business Review, 1983, pp. 30-50.
3. *Oxford Advanced Learners Dictionary*, Oxford University Press, 7th Edition, 2007, p. 687.
4. Francis Cherunilam, *Business Policy and Strategic Management*, Himalaya Publishing House, Mumbai, 2006, p. 183.
5. Khan, M.Y., Jain, P.K., *Financial Management*, TATA McGraw Hill Publications, New Delhi, 2006, pp. 715-716.
6. Helfer, E.A., *Technology of Financial Analysis*, Irwin Home Wood Ill, 1972, p. 53.
7. *Ibid*., p. 56.
8. Berndts, E., Morrison, J., *Capacity Utilisation Measures Underlying Economic Theory — An Alternative Approach*, American Economic Review, 1981, pp. 48-52.
9. Kothari, C.R., *Research Methodology*, New Age International Publishers, New Delhi, 2007, p. 316.
10. Altman E.I., *The Success of Business Failure Prediction Models—An International Survey*, Journal of Banking and Finance, 1984, 8(12): pp. 171-197.
11. *Op.cit*., pp. 171-197.

Entrepreneurship and Growth *Relationship Analysis*

INTRODUCTION

In developing economies entrepreneurship plays a leading role in the process of industrial development, Entrepreneurship is an attempt to create value through recognition of business opportunity[1]. Entrepreneurship is a dynamic process involving fusion of capital, technology and human talent. Therefore, an entrepreneur is looked upon as a talented person capable of assuming risk, marshalling the necessary resources needed for the business. Above all, the entrepreneurs have an insight to go in for innovations and adapting to the fast changing circumstances. The entrepreneur perceives a need and then brings together the manpower, materials and capital required to meet that need. Further, the entrepreneur foresees the potentially profitable opportunity and tries to exploit it. Thus the entrepreneur initiates changes and innovation. Entrepreneur is the backbone of any industry in its growth. Growth of an institution mainly depends upon the entrepreneur and his/her talents. Entrepreneurial growth and industrial growth are closely related. History reveals that many of the industrial units have failed down only because of the deficiency in entrepreneurship. Hence, this chapter attempts to probe the relationship between entrepreneurial variables and growth in fishnet units in Kanyakumari district.

Primary data collected from the fishnet units through the structured questionnaire have been used to the study the relationship between entrepreneurship and the growth of fishnet units in Kanyakumari district.

ENTREPRENEURSHIP

The term 'Entrepreneur' and 'Entrepreneurship' are often used interchangeably. But, they are conceptually different. The word 'Entrepreneur' is derived from the French word 'Enterprendre' meaning 'to undertake'. In fact, in the 16th century, the French men who undertook military expeditions were referred to as 'Entrepreneurs'. Later on, in the 18th century, this term got associated with persons who started their own enterprises. Richard Cantillon, an Irish man living in France, was the first Economist who introduced the term 'entrepreneur' referring to the risk taking function of establishing a new venture[2].

Generally speaking, entrepreneur refers to a person who establishes his own business or industrial undertaking with a view to making profit. An entrepreneur is considered to be the originator of a business venture. He takes the role of an organiser in the process of production. An entrepreneur perceives a need to start an organisation and then brings together the manpower, materials, and capital required to meet the need. He searches for change, responds to it and exploits it as an opportunity.

Various experts have defined the term entrepreneur in different words. Some of the definitions run as: According to Collins Cobuild English Language Dictionary, (1987) explains that, "an entrepreneur is a person who sets up business, deals in order to make a profit". According to J.B. Say[3], "an entrepreneur is the economic agent who unites all means of production and who finds in value of the products". Richard Cantillon[4] says, that "All persons engaged in economic activity are entrepreneurs" In the words of Quesnay[5], "A rich farmer is an entrepreneur who manages and makes his business profitable by his intelligence and wealth". J.A. Schumpeter[6] is of the view that, "A person who introduces innovative changes is an entrepreneur and he is an integral part of economic growth'. According to Webster[7], "Entrepreneur is one who assumes risk and management of business". In the words of Walker[8], "True entrepreneur is one who is endowed with more than average capacities in the risk of organising and coordinating various factors of production" Peter Drucker[9] says that "entrepreneur is one who always searches for change, responds to it and exploits it as an opportunity. Innovation is a specific tool of entrepreneurs, the means by which they exploit change as an opportunity for different business or service". Dewing[10] has rightly put it as, "the functions of entrepreneur is one that promotes ideas into business".

Thus, an entrepreneur is always action oriented with the entrepreneurial ability. The entrepreneur visualises the necessary steps involved from idea generation to its actualisation. The entrepreneur is both a thinker and doer otherwise planner and worker. In carrying out the business, an entrepreneur accepts risk and manages it.

FUNCTIONS OF ENTREPRENEURS

An entrepreneur is an agent who brings various factors of production with a view to make and offer products and services which can be sold in the market. While doing so, the entrepreneur performs the following basic functions:

Risk Assumption Function: An entrepreneur necessarily acts as 'risk bearing' agent of production since he has to bear a greater amount of uncertainties in business. The term uncertainty refers to more than an ordinary risk which can be measured and insured. The risk that an entrepreneur bears includes the uncertainty that cannot be insured and incalculable. For instancc, risk due to possibility of changes in the taste of customers, changes in fashion and technique of production, new inventions and the like cannot be insured. But, an entrepreneur has to undertake and face such uncertainties. The entrepreneur assumes this risk and tries to reduce these uncertainties by his/her initiative, skill and ability.

Decision Making Function: From the very inception of the business till its development, an entrepreneur takes decisions at various stages. Further, the entrepreneur decides the nature and type of goods to be produced, the size of the business, its location, technique of production and the like. A successful entrepreneur is one who takes sound decisions at the appropriate time so that the business succeeds.

Managerial Function: An entrepreneur performs the managerial function also. Managerial functions include the functions like coordination, organisation, and supervision. An entrepreneur is one who combines the land of one, the labour of another and the capital of yet another, and produces a product. While undertaking an enterprise, the entrepreneur performs all managerial functions starting with planning and ending with controlling.

Innovation Function: Innovation is an important function of an entrepreneur. In this context, the distinction between an investor and an innovator is needed to be clarified. The person who discovers new methods, new materials and machines is called an inventor. But the person who utilises these inventions so as to make new combination of products is called an innovator. Innovation is a never ending process and in fact, it is an ongoing function. Thus, an entrepreneur always looks on to introduce a new product or a new production technology or open a new market hitherto untapped or discover a new source of supply of new material. Innovators are always successful in their ventures.

ENTREPRENEURSHIP

Entrepreneurship like many other economic concepts has long been debated. It has been define and used in various ways and in various senses.

It is an exclusive concept that can not be defined precisely. The word 'entrepreneurship' has been derived from the French word which means 'to undertake'. Today people call it by various names such as 'adventurism', 'risk taking', 'thrill seeking', 'innovating' and the like.

The term 'entrepreneurship' also has different definitions. According to Benjamin Higgins, "Entrepreneurship means the function of foreseeing investment and production opportunity, organizing an enterprise to undertake a new production process, raising capital, hiring labour, arranging the supply of raw-materials, finding site, introducing a new technique and commodities, discovering new sources of raw- materials and selecting top managers of day-to-day operations of the enterprise"[11].

In a Conference on 'Entrepreneurship' held at United States of America in 1989 the term entrepreneurship was defined as, "the attempt to create value through recognition of business opportunity, the management of risk-taking appropriate to the opportunity, and through the communicative and management skills to mobilise human, financial, and material resources necessary to bring a project to fruition"[12].

According to Diamond, "entrepreneurship is equivalent to 'enterprise' which involves the willingness to assume risks in undertaking an economic activity particularly a new one. It involves an innovation but not necessarily so. It always involves risk-taking and decision-making, although neither risk nor decision making is of great significance"[13].

According to A.H. Cole, "Entrepreneurship is the purposeful activity of an individual or a group of associated individuals, undertaken to initiate, maintain or aggrandise profit by production or distribution of economic goods and services"[14].

According to Schumpeter[15], "Entrepreneurship is based on purposeful and systematic innovation". In the words of McClelland[16], "Entrepreneurship involves doing things in a new and better way. It calls for decision making under uncertainty. If there is no significant uncertainty and the action involves applying known and predictable results, then entrepreneurship is not at all involved".

Entrepreneurship can be viewed as a creative and innovative response to the environment and an ability to recognise, initiate and exploit an economic opportunity. Thus entrepreneurship is a process involving various functions to be undertaken to establish an enterprise.

CHARACTERISTICS OF ENTREPRENEURSHIP

The characteristics of entrepreneurship that can be inferred from the above definitions are:

(i) Innovation

(ii) Risk bearing

(iii) Decision making

(iv) Organisation and management

(v) Making the enterprise a success

(vi) Accepting challenges

(vii) Handling economic uncertainty

(viii) Problem solving

(ix) Opportunity seeking

(x) Systematic planning

Of the above, innovation and risk bearing are considered to be the two basic but important elements of entrepreneurship.

Innovation: Entrepreneurship has innovation as its hallmark. Doing something new or something different is a prerequisite for entrepreneurship. Entrepreneurs are constantly doing something new and different to meet the changing requirements of customers. Even if they are not the inventors of new products, they have the capacity to apply these inventions for the benefit of their enterprises and also the customers.

Risk bearing: Entrepreneurship necessarily involves risk bearing since doing something new and different is always risky. Starting an enterprise does not guarantee profits always. There is every possibility to incur losses due to severe competition, change in government policies and customers, preferences, shortage of labour and raw material and the like. Inspite of this, entrepreneurs come forward boldly to assume risk and start enterprises of their own and manage them. The risk bearing ability enables the entrepreneur to carry on their business or industry, even if they fail in one or two occasions, hoping that they would succeed ultimately.

FACTORS STIMULATING ENTREPRENEURSHIP

There are many factors which induce prospective entrepreneurs to take up some productive ventures or other. These factors act as 'stimulants' for falling up entreprerurial activity and thereby generating economic development in the country. The factors stimulating entrepreneurship are:

(i) Capital formation — making capital available to entrepreneurs to start new ventures.

(ii) Entrepreneurship Development Programmes — supportive Government programmes to develop entrepreneurship.

(iii) *Training facilities* — availability of adequate training facilities to promote and develop entrepreneurship.

(iv) *Suitable environment* — to transform scientific and technical development into economically viable projects.

(v) *Collateral arrangement* — to establish a cordial relationship between business and research to carry transferability of technology to the market place.

(vi) *Ideal climate for innovation* — to promote and develop entrepreneurial activities.

ENTREPRENEUR *VS.* ENTREPRENEURSHIP

The term 'entrepreneur' is equally important as the term 'entrepreneurship'. Though these two terms are two sides of the some coin, conceptually they are different. While 'entrepreneur' refers to a person, 'entrepreneurship' refers to the function which the entrepreneur performs. Basically, entrepreneur in a business is the leader and the functions performed by him/her in relation to that business is entrepreneurship. The relationship between entrepreneur and entrepreneurship can be best explained as below:

Relationship between Entrepreneur and Entrepreneurship

Entrepreneur	Entrepreneurship
Person	Function/Process
Organiser	Organisation
Innovator	Innovation
Motivator	Motivation
Leader	Leadership
Creator	Creation
Risk - bearer	Risk-Bearing
Initiator	Initiative
Visualise	Vision
Technician	Technology
Imitator	Imitation
Administrator	Administration

THEORIES OF ENTREPRENEURSHIP

The concept entrepreneurship and its theories have been evolved over a period of more than two centuries. There are different opinions on the emergence of entrepreneurship. These opinions are classified into three categories.

The Economists View: In Economics, entrepreneurship and economic growth take place in those situations where particular economic conditions are most favorable. G.F. Papanek and J.R. Harris are the main advocates of this theory. According to them economic incentives are the main drive for the entrepreneurial activities. In some cases, it is not so evident, but the persons' with inner drives have always been associated with economic gains. Therefore, these incentives and gains are regarded as the sufficient condition for the emergence of industrial entrepreneurship[17]. When an individual recognises that the market for a product or service is out of equilibrium, he/she may purchase the product at the prevailing price and sell to those who are prepared to buy at the highest price[18]. Lack of vigorous entrepreneurship is due to various kinds of market imperfections and inefficient economic policies.

Sociological Theory: Sociologists argue that entrepreneurship is most likely to emerge under a specific social culture. According to them, social sanctions, cultural values and role expectations are responsible for the emergence of entrepreneurship. According to Cochran[19] the entrepreneur represents society's model personality. Entrepreneurs performance depends upon their own attitudes towards his occupation, the role expectations of sanctioning groups and the occupational requirements of the job. Society's values are the most important determinants of the attitudes and role expectations. According to Weber[20], religious beliefs produce intensive exertion in occupational pursuits, the systematic ordering of means to end, and the accumulation of assets. It is these beliefs which generate a drive for entrepreneurial growth. Hoselitz suggests that culturally marginal groups promote entrepreneurship and economic development. Such groups because of their ambiguous position peculiarly suited to make creative adjustments and thereby develop genuine innovation[21]. In several countries, entrepreneurs have emerged from a particular socio-economic class[22]. The protestant ethic of the west is said to have contributed to the emergence of a new class of industrialists. In Britan, the United States of America and Turkey, ranks of entrepreneurs were filled from commerce. The Samurai in Japan, Family Patter in France, Yoruba in Nigeria, Kikuyu in Kenya, Christians in Lebanon, Halimenon in Pakistan, Marwaris and Parsees in India are considered to be the dominant social classes of entrepreneurs. In the study of the origin and background of entrepreneurs in several countries, Hagen[23] concluded that entrepreneurs have emerged from certain communities and castes.

According to Stokes, socio-cultural values channel economic action. He suggests that personal and societal opportunity and the presence of the requisite psychological distributions are the conditions to move an individual into industrial entrepreneur[24].

Psychological Theory: According to the advocates of this theory, entrepreneurship is most likely to emerge when a society has sufficient supply of individuals possessing particular psychological characteristics. Schumpeter believes that entrepreneurs are primarily motivated by an atavistic will power, will to found a private kingdom or will to conquer. The main characteristics of entrepreneurs are:

(a) an institutional capacity to see things in a way which afterwards proves correct;

(b) energy to overcome fixed habits of thought; and

(c) the capacity to withstand social opposition[25]

According to McCelland, it is high need for achievement which drives people towards entrepreneurial activities. This achievement motive is included through child rearing practices, which stress standards of excellence, material warmth, self-reliance training and low father dominance. Individuals with high achievement motive trend to take keen interest in situations of high risk desire for responsibility and a desire for a concrete measure of task performance[26]. Hagen considers withdrawal of status respect as the trigger mechanism for change in personality formation. Status withdrawal is the perception on the part of the members of some social group that their purposes and values in life are not represented by groups in the society whom they respect and whose esteem they value. Hagen identifies four types of events that can produce status withdrawal:

(a) displacement by force;

(b) denigration of valued symbols;

(c) inconsistency of status symbols with a changing distribution of economic power; and

(d) non-acceptance of expected status on migration to a new society[27].

Kunkel's behavioural model is concerned with the overtly expressed activities of individuals and their relations to the previously and presently surrounding social structures and physical conditions[28]. Behavioural patterns in this model are determined by reinforcing and aversive stimuli present in the social context. Hence, entrepreneurial behaviour is a function of the surrounding social structure, both past and present and can be readily influenced by the manipulative economic and social incentives.

Each of the above theories is incomplete and none of them is right or wrong. Entrepreneurship is influenced by a multitude of factors and therefore, no single factor by itself can generate entrepreneurship. Thus, entrepreneurship is the outcome of a complex and varying combinations of socio-economic, psychological and other factors.

ENTREPRENEURSHIP AND GROWTH

The entrepreneur turns a business idea into reality, either by starting a new business or by injecting new life into an old one. A good and efficient entrepreneur successfully run an industrial enterprise and achieves growth. Even the loss making business units could be made potentially viable if the entrepreneurs are so efficient. Thus entrepreneurship and growth of industrial unit are closely related to one another.

Entrepreneurship is a complex phenomenon which depends upon many, socio-economic, psychological and personal variables related to entrepreneurs. The psychological variables such as individual habits, attitudes, their perceptions and their personality traits determine the entrepreneurship qualities and their performance.

The researcher has identified ten such pertinent variables as related to the growth of fishnet units. The variables identified for analysis are: community of the entrepreneurs, nature of ownership, religion of the entrepreneurs, reasons for starting the fishnet unit, varieties of products manufactured, owned capital invested, number of machineries installed, number of work shifts in fishnet units, period of establishment and forms of organisation. These entrepreneurial variables have significant role in the determination of entrepreneurial performance vis-à-vis industrial growth.

RELATIONSHIP BETWEEN ENTREPRENEURSHIP AND GROWTH

The role of entrepreneurs on the growth of fishnet units is of paramount importance. The growth of the fishnet unit mainly depends upon its entrepreneur. The personal variables related to the entrepreneurs have a direct relationship with the growth achieved by the entrepreneurs. The history of the fishnet units which have become sick and closed down reveals the fact that these units have become sick and failed down only because of the inefficient management of the institution by its entrepreneurs. Similarly, many of the ill managed fishnet units resulted into loss for years together have shown progress and profit in course of time when they are acquired by a new entrepreneurs with high entrepreneurial talent. Many of the present fishnet units showing growth in recent times have been so acquired for lease or purchased outright by the present entrepreneurs from the former entrepreneurs, who lack entrepreneurship. In Kanyakumari district the researcher has observed many such entrepreneurs. Hence, only because of the entrepreneurial efficiency a group of fishnet units is able to achieve growth and the others could not so achieve because of their deficiencies. The foregoing discussion in the chapter examines the relationship that exists between the entrepreneurial variable and the growth achieved by the entrepreneurs in fishnet industry.

COMMUNITY

Community is the social segregation and stratification of people into different groups. From time immemorial, Indian society has been fragmented into different groups called community or caste. Everyone in the Indian society is identified to be associated with some community. It is an artificial categorization attached with everyone in the society by birth and switch over from one community to another is not allowed and permitted and even not recognised. In recent times even though cutting the traditional barbarian block many inter caste marriages are arranged, the children of the couples are recognised with either the father's community or mother's community. So even the inter caste or community marriage did not crash the community bar. Thus, community or caste still continues to be an important factor determining the social setting of the people in India. There are thousands of communities and sub-communities in India. Some communities confine to a particular area or district or state while the others have a wider base. Each community has different cultural and customary practices which are completely different from the others. Even the language, food and dressing pattern differ among communities. Those attached to particular community have a close affinity with the members belonging to the same community. There are associations even political outfits to protect and promote each community. The ugly scene one could more frequently see in many underdeveloped economies is the personal clashes between two communities. Even for no reasons, the members of different communities clash with others. India records such sort of vandalism in innumerable numbers.

In India from Vedic times to till date different jobs have been exclusively reserved for specific communities. In Vedic period society was divided into four communities. They are Brahmins, Shatriyas, Sutras and Vaisyas. Each community was allowed to perform a specified job only. Any violation was viewed as a taboo and hard punishments were assigned for such violations. But in course of time such barbarian restrictions on job were removed. Hence, now any one is allowed to do any job as he/she likes. But still many jobs are identified with specific communities. Now eventhough absolutely there is no restriction on doing any job for any one, there are few jobs exclusively or mainly carried out by people belonging to a few specified communities. In Tamil Nadu, the Vishwakarma community is identified with blacksmithy and goldsmithy, the Nadars are identified with Palmyra climbing and the Chettiar community is associated with financing.

In the same way communities like Paravas and Mukkuvas are identified with fishing. Fishing has been the primary occupation of these communities. In recent times many entrepreneurs belonging to other communities have also entered in the fishing arena. Eventhough fishing is carried out mainly by fishermen; many others belonging to other communities have also entered in the field especially in fishery related activities. Both fishermen and non fishermen are engaged in fishery industry. In the same way fishnet industry is run by entrepreneurs belonging to fishermen and non fishermen communities.

Since fishing is a traditional occupation of fishermen community, entrepreneurs hailing from fishermen community are well exposed to the practices of fisheries. Since entrepreneurs belonging to fishermen community undertake fishing from childhood they are well versed with fishery related businesses. So, many of the entrepreneurs belonging to fishermen community have wonderfully succeeded in these businesses. In fishery, entrepreneurs belonging to other communities other than fishermen find hard to succeed. Because of this, entrepreneurs belonging to other communities, other than fishermen are not familiar with fishing practices.

In fishnet industry, fishnet manufacturing units are run by entrepreneurs belonging to fishermen community and other communities. The progress and growth achieved by entrepreneurs belonging to both of these communities are different. The growth achieved by entrepreneurs of these communities is analysed in this part. Table 4.1 shows the community-wise classification of entrepreneurs in fishnet units in Kanyakumari district.

Table 4.1: Community-wise Classification of Entrepreneurs

Sl. No.	Community	Number of Entrepreneurs	Percentage
1.	Fishermen	21	24.14
2.	Non-Fishermen	66	75.86
	Total	**87**	**100.00**

Source: Primary data.

It is observed from the Table 4.1 that 75.86 per cent (66 fishnet units) of the total 87 fishnet units are run by non fishermen entrepreneurs in Kanyakumari district. Another 21 fishnet units out of 87 units (24.14%) are belonging to entrepreneurs from fishermen community. Thus it is clearly observed that majority of the fishnet units run in Kanyakumari district belongs to entrepreneurs belonging to non fishermen community. Hence, it can be concluded that fishnet manufacturing is not carried out by entrepreneurs belonging to fishermen community alone. The reasons for this trend may be that fishnet industry of the day is not a traditional business. Modern fishnet industry replaced the traditional manual fishnet manufacturing by machines. Further, starting up of a fishnet unit requires technical knowledge about manpower, machineries, materials, marketing and finance, which the traditional fishermen lack. Only those entrepreneurs from fishermen community with the above said talents and with sufficient finance can succeed in this business. Hence, many of the traditional manual fishnet manufacturers from fishermen community have not entered into this modern fishnet industry and started their units.

Further, in Kanyakumari district 74 per cent of the total population is non-fishermen. They mainly depend upon agriculture. No major industry has been started by them. The growth of fishnet units in the district prompted them to start many more fishnet units. Grabing this business opportunity now many fishnet units have been started by entrepreneurs belonging to non-fishermen community. Hence, now fishnet manufacturing is dominated by entrepreneurs belonging to non-fishermen community.

Since the growth achieved by the fishnet units has a relationship with the communal setting of the entrepreneurs, a two way table representing the community setting of the entrepreneurs and the growth achieved by them is prepared. The Table 4.2 analyses the relationship between the growth of the fishnet units and communal setting, related to entrepreneurs. The growth calculated through the growth scale discussed in the former chapter has been used for analysis.

Table 4.2: Community-wise Classification of Entrepreneurs and Growth of Fishnet Units

Community	Status of Growth				Total	
	Growth		Non-Growth			
	No. of Units	Percentage	No. of Units	Percentage	No. of Units	Percentage
Fishermen	5	24	16	76	21	100
Non-fishermen	31	47	35	53	66	100
Total	**36**		**51**		**87**	**100**

Source: Primary data.

The two way Table 4.2 shows that 16 fishnet units (76%) out of 21 fishnet units run by fishermen entrepreneurs have recorded non-growth and the remaining 5 fishnet units (24%) have recorded growth. Further, the analysis clearly reveals that 35 fishnet units out of 66 units (53%) run by the entrepreneurs belonging to non-fishermen community are found to be non-growth units and the remaining, 47 per cent (31 fishnet units) have recorded growth. It shows that among the fishermen community only 24 per cent have achieved growth while among the entrepreneurs belonging to non-fishermen community 47 per cent have achieved growth. Hence, it can be concluded that entrepreneurs belonging to non-fishermen community have achieved a better growth in fishnet industry than the entrepreneurs belonging to fishermen community.

In order to statistically test the relationship between the variables namely community of the entrepreneurs and the growth achieved by their fishnet units, Chi-square test is applied. For applying Chi-square test, the following null hypothesis is fixed.

H_o : There is no significant difference in growth among fishnet units run by entrepreneurs belonging to fishermen and non-fishermen communities in Kanyakumari district.

The alternative hypothesis is

H_a : There is significant difference in growth among fishnet units run by entrepreneurs belonging to fishermen and non-fishermen communities in Kanyakumari district.

The findings of the Chi-square test are presented in Table 4.3.

Table 4.3: Relationship Between Community and Growth-Chi-square Test

Relationship	O	E	O - E	$(O - E)^2$	$(O - E)^2/E$
$R_1 C_1$	5	8.69	-3.69	13.62	1.57
$R_2 C_1$	31	12.31	18.69	349.32	28.38
$R_1 C_2$	16	27.31	-11.31	127.92	4.68
$R_2 C_2$	35	38.69	-3.69	13.62	0.35
Calculated Value					**34.98**

Source: Primary data.

df = 1

Table value at 5% level is 3.84.

Since the calculated value is higher (34.98) than the Table value (3.84), the null hypothesis is rejected and the alternative hypothesis is accepted. Hence, it is concluded that there is significant difference in growth achieved by entrepreneurs belonging to fishermen community and other communities. This implies that the community is a major variable which has a significant relationship with the growth of fishnet units.

RELIGION

Religion plays a vital role in the personal and social life of the people. Each religion has a separate value system, which is different from other religion. Each religion has different faith and belief. In India different religions are practised in different parts of the country. The popular religions which have more followers in the country are Hinduism, Christianity, Islam, Jainism,

Zoroastrianism, Parsism and Sikhism. Each religion has its own Holy books and God/Goddess. The Holy books and preaching of God/Goddess and religious heads positively motivate their followers to grow further in their personal/business/official life. Each religion preaches peace and love. The followers of each religion strictly follow the preaching of their religious head/heads. Every violation to this preaching is treated as evil. Those who have faith in their religion strictly adhere to it. The followers of a particular religion who are running the business develop their business on the lines of their religion. Similarly, one could see that many businessmen belonging to Islam, run their business on the lines of *'shariat'*, the law book of Islam. The caste systems prevailing in Hinduism disallow the cast Hindus (Brahmins) to start and run business. This shows that the religion has a bearing on the growth of entrepreneurship. Hence, it is decided to probe the relationship between religion and growth of the entrepreneurship.

Fisheries and allied activities are not confined to any specific religion or community in India. However, in most parts of Tamil Nadu fishing activities are exclusively done by fishermen community consisting of various sub castes whereas the other allied activities related to fishing are done by people belonging to various other communities. Fishnet industry, an allied activity of fisheries, is run by entrepreneurs belonging to fishermen and non-fishermen communities. In Kanyakumari district, it is significant to note that, the entire fishermen population is belonging to a single religion-Christianity. However, the fishnet industry is not confined to Christian religion alone in the district. Entrepreneurs belonging to Hinduism and Islam have also entered in the fishnet industry. As pointed out earlier, it has been observed that there is a relationship between the growth of fishnet industry and the religion to which the entrepreneur belongs.

Table 4.4 exhibits the details of fishnet units by the religious setting of its entrepreneurs.

Table 4.4: Classification of Entrepreneurs by Religion

Sl. No.	Religion	Number of Entrepreneurs	Percentage
1.	Hindu	15	17.24
2.	Christian	56	64.37
3.	Islam	16	18.39
	Total	87	**100.00**

Source: Primary data.

Table 4.4 shows that among the total respondents, 64.37 per cent in Kanyakumari district are belonging to Christianity (56 entrepreneurs out of 87 fishnet units). Another 16 entrepreneurs (18.39 per cent) are belonging to

Islam and rests of the 17.29 per cent entrepreneurs in the study area are Hindus. Hence, the researcher observed that most of the entrepreneurs in fishnet units of Kanyakumari district belong to Christianity.

In order to study the relationship between the growth achieved by the fishnet units and religious setting of the entrepreneurs in fishnet industry, a two way table representing the relationship between the religion of the entrepreneurs and the growth achieved by them is prepared and presented in Table 4.5.

Table 4.5: Religion-wise Classification of Entrepreneurs and Growth

Religion	Status of Growth				Total	
	Growth		Non-Growth			
	No. of Units	Percentage	No. of Units	Percentage	No. of Units	Percentage
Hinduism	3	20.00	12	80.00	15	100
Christianity	28	50.00	28	50.00	56	100
Islam	5	31.25	11	68.75	16	100
Total	**36**		**51**		**87**	**100**

Source: Primary data.

From the above Table 4.5 it is observed that among the fishnet units run by the entrepreneurs belonging to Hinduism, 80 per cent (12 units out of 15 fishnet units) have recorded non-growth and 20 per cent of the fishnet units (3 units) have recorded growth. Among the fishnet units run by Christian entrepreneurs, the growth and non-growth units are equal in number (28 fishnet units each). Further analysis shows that out of 16 fishnet units run by the Muslim entrepreneurs, 11 units (68.75%) have become non-growth units and the remaining 31.25 per cent (5 units) have recorded growth.

Thus it is clear that the growth units and non-growth units are equal in case of Christian entrepreneurs and it is very low among the Hindu entrepreneurs. In case of Muslim entrepreneurs, nearly one-third of the units run by them have recorded growth. Thus the growth is comparatively higher among the Christian entrepreneurs than the entrepreneurs belonging to other religions.

In order to observe the relationship between the variables such as religion of the entrepreneurs and the growth achieved by their units, Chi-square test is applied. For applying Chi-square test the following null hypothesis is fixed.

H_0 : There is no significant difference in the growth of fishnet units among entrepreneurs belonging to Hinduism, Islam and Christianity.

The alternative hypothesis is:

H_a : There is significant difference in the growth of fishnet units among entrepreneurs belonging to Hinduism, Islam and Christianity.

The finding of the Chi-square test is presented in Table 4.6.

Table 4.6: Relationship between Religion and Growth-Chi-Square Test

Relationship	O	E	O - E	$(O - E)^2$	$(O - E)^2/E$
$R_1 C_1$	3	6.21	-3.21	10.30	1.66
$R_1 C_2$	28	23.17	4.83	23.33	1.01
$R_1 C_3$	5	6.62	-1.62	2.62	0.40
$R_2 C_1$	12	8.79	3.21	10.30	1.17
$R_3 C_3$	11	9.38	1.62	2.62	0.28
Calculated Value					5.23

Source: Primary data.

df = 2

Table value at 5% level is 5.991.

Since the calculated value is less (5.23) than the table value (5.991) the null hypothesis is accepted. Hence, it is concluded that there is no significant difference in growth of fishnet units among the entrepreneurs of different religions. So it shows that the religion of the entrepreneurs is not a major variable which has a relationship with growth.

REASONS FOR STARTING THE UNIT

Every human activity has a reason or motive behind it. In business, profit is the ultimate motive for which every activity is carried out. The desire to earn profit is no doubt an important motivating force to an entrepreneur and reason behind starting a business. However, entrepreneurs are not purely motivated by profit alone. There are several internal and external factors or reasons that motivate the entrepreneurs to start their business enterprise. Possession of occupational skill and experience, the need for self employment, family/social compulsion, are the most common reasons or motives for entering into a business in addition to their profit motive for doing business. The experiences accumulated either as executives in industrial concerns or traders, merchants motivate the entrepreneurs to start and grow a business. An occupational skill associated with experience provides confidence to the entrepreneurs and serves as the important motivating factor. Many times, it is the compulsion rather than the ambitions, which leads a man to success. The compulsions such as the need for continuing a family business or supporting family members in their business often become a reason for entering into business. Such compulsion may arise in the form of need for self employment. A considerable number of people have become entrepreneurs just because of lack of any other employment opportunities. Some may choose self-employment to capitalise their skills and business experience for themselves than working for others. As the motive behind and reason for starting a business is a source of influence and motivation to entrepreneurs, it contributes much towards the growth of business enterprise.

It is observed in the study that occupational experience, the need for self- employment and family compulsion are the common reasons for starting a fishnet unit in Kanyakumari district. The occupational experience refers to the experience of the entrepreneurs in the same industry as workers, supervisors, technicians, managers, sales representatives and merchants in the similar lines in other industrial units.

The reasons for starting fishnet units in Kanyakumari district as observed by the respondents is presented in Table 4.7.

Table 4.7: Reasons for Starting Fishnet Units

Sl. No.	Reasons	Number of Entrepreneurs	Percentage
1.	Experience in the business	24	27.59
2.	Self- employment	36	41.38
3.	Compulsion from family	27	31.03
	Total	**87**	**100.00**

Source: Primary data.

Table 4.7 clearly explains that the majority of the fishnet units, 36 units out of 87 fishnet units (41.38 per cent), have been started by the entrepreneurs with the intention of self employment. Another 24 fishnet units have been started by the entrepreneurs to capitalise their business experience and the remaining 27 fishnet units (31.03%) have been started out of compulsion from family situations.

Thus, it can be concluded that only less than one third of the entrepreneurs have started their units out of compulsions and majority of the entrepreneurs have started their units with real entrepreneurial spirit such as to be self-employed and capitalising their previous experience.

It is observed that the growth achieved by the fishnet units and the various reasons for starting the industrial units by the entrepreneurs have a direct relationship with one another. Therefore a two way table representing the relationship between the reason for starting the fishnet units and the growth achieved by them is prepared and presented in Table 4.8.

Table 4.8: Reasons for Starting the Units and Growth

Reasons	Status of Growth				Total	
	Growth		Non-Growth			
	No. of Units	Percentage	No. of Units	Percentage	No. of Units	Percentage
Experience in the business	14	58.33	10	41.67	24	100
Self-employment	15	41.66	21	58.34	36	100
Compulsion from family	7	25.93	20	74.07	27	100
Total	**36**		**51**		**87**	**100**

Source: Primary data.

Table 4.8 shows that out of 24 fishnet units run by the entrepreneurs with the previous experience, 58.33 per cent (14 fishnet units) have registered growth and 41.67 per cent (10 units) of the fishnet units have become non-growth. Among the total of 36 fishnet units started with the intention of self-employment, 15 fishnet units (41.66%) have registered growth and 21 fishnet units (58.34%) have not registered growth. Among the 27 fishnet units started out of family compulsions, only 7 fishnet units have recorded growth and 20 fishnet units have not shown any growth.

Thus, it is observed that the growth is high among the fishnet units started by the entrepreneurs with previous experience in the business and it is very low among the units started by the entrepreneurs out of family compulsions.

In order to examine the relationship among the variables, reasons for starting the fishnet industrial units and their growth, Chi-square test was applied. For applying Chi-square test the following null hypothesis is fixed.

H_o : There is no significant difference in the growth among fishnet units promoted by entrepreneurs for different reasons.

The alternative hypothesis is:

H_a : There is significant difference in the growth among fishnet units promoted by entrepreneurs for different reasons.

The finding of the chi-square test is presented in Table 4.9.

Table 4.9: Relationship between Reasons for Starting the Unit and Growth-Chi-square test

Relationship	O	E	O - E	$(O - E)^2$	$(o - E)^{2/E}$
$R_1 C_1$	14	9.93	4.07	16.56	1.68
$R_1 C_2$	15	14.90	0.10	0.01	0.00
$R_1 C_3$	7	11.17	-4.17	17.39	1.56
$R_2 C_1$	10	14.07	-4.07	16.56	1.18
$R_2 C_2$	21	21.10	-0.10	0.01	0.00
$R_2 C_3$	20	15.83	4.17	17.39	1.10
Calculated Value					5.52

Source: Primary data.

df = 2

Table value at 5% level is 5.991.

Since the calculated value is less (5.52) than the table value (5.991), the null hypothesis is accepted. Hence, it is concluded that there is no significant difference in growth achieved by entrepreneurs with different reasons for starting the fishnet industrial units. So it shows that the reasons for starting the fishnet units is not a major variable having a relationship with the growth.

NATURE OF OWNERSHIP

A business can be started in different ways. The first way is that an entrepreneur himself/herself can take an initiative by forming an industrial unit by investing his/her own fund or by mobilising finance from his/her friends and relatives or by borrowing funds from banks and financial institutions. The entrepreneur has to search for funds and arrange them in his/her own interest from different sources. After identifying a suitable location in consultation with experts and owners of existing units he/she has to build his unit. It requires a huge and long term investment.

The other way to start an industrial unit is to hire another surviving unit for rent. In this case, the entrepreneur is heavily relieved from the burden of long-term financial commitment. Instead he/she is needed to invest only in short term investments such as working capital related requirements. So a small amount of money alone is needed for the entrepreneurs. All expenses what he/she incurs are related to production. Only a small amount of rent he/she has to pay either monthly or weekly or quarterly or on in any other form as may be agreed. Hence, the commitment required from the entrepreneur is very low in this option.

The third option is to start an industrial unit is acquiring a running business for lease. The entrepreneur has to search for industrial units which are not able to be run by the entrepreneurs for different reasons and acquire such units for lease. The entrepreneur need not invest money in fixed assets. Only a small amount of money required to carry out production is needed to be invested in the business.

Industrial units started in these three categories are poised for growth. The entrepreneurs who own the industrial units from their own fund show better performance than others. Since they have started the industrial unit on their own fund, they need to bear only the running expenses. They have no fixed expenditure like rent or lease amount. Further, as it is his/her own business, any thing which is good or bad, to his business will personally affect him/her. This makes them to achieve a higher growth in their business. But the other two categories of entrepreneurs will not be as serious and enthusiastic as they always feel that they run a unit which is not belonging to them. They always think about maintaining the business and earning profit. Further, they have a thinking that at any time the business could be taken back by their owners. Hence, such enterprises can not show better growth than the units started and owned by the owners themselves. So, there is a wide variation between the growth achieved by entrepreneurs started business with their own funds and with others.

As in any other business, in fishnet units in Kanyakumari district there are three types of entrepreneur, such as owners, lessees, and tenants. The detail of the fishnet units by the type of ownership is presented in Table 4.10.

Table 4.10: Type of Ownership of Business

Sl. No.	Type	Number of Entrepreneurs	Percentage
1.	Owned	65	74.71
2.	Rental	15	17.24
3.	Lease	7	8.05
	Total	**87**	**100.00**

Source: Primary data.

Table 4.10 reveals that out of 87 fishnet units, as its high 65 fishnet units (74.71%) are owned establishments of the entrepreneurs. Next to the owned ones, there are 15 fishnet units (17.24%) which are hired from others by the present entrepreneurs and a very minimum of 8.05 per cent (7 units out of 87 fishnet units) units are run on lease. Thus, around three-fourth of the fishnet units are owned establishments of the entrepreneurs.

It is observed that the growth achieved by the fishnet units and the type of ownership of the enterprise have a direct relationship. Therefore, a two way table representing the relationship between ownership of the enterprise and the growth achieved by the entrepreneurs is prepared and presented in Table 4.11.

Table 4.11: Pattern of Ownership and Growth of Fishnet Units

Ownership	Status of Growth				Total	
	Growth		Non-Growth			
	No. of Units	Percentage	No. of Units	Percentage	No. of Units	Percentage
Owned	26	40.00	39	60.00	65	100
Hired	8	53.33	7	46.67	15	100
Leased	2	28.57	5	71.43	7	100
Total	**36**		**51**		**87**	**100**

Source: Primary data.

Table 4.11 exhibits the categorization of the growth and non-growth fishnet units in Kanyakumari district based on the ownership pattern. It is clearly observed that 60 per cent of total 65 owned fishnet unit studied are found to be non-growth units and 26 fishnet units (40%) have achieved growth. Another set of 8 fishnet units out of 15 hired units (53.33%) have achieved growth and 46.67 per cent units (7 fishnet units) have not achieved growth. Further analysis reveals that among 7 leased units, 5 fishnet units (71.43%) have not shown growth and only 2 of the leased units (28.57%) have become growth units in Kanyakumari district.

Thus, it is clear that the growth in terms of number of units is high in case of hired fishnet units and it is low among the leased units. It is significant to note that the growth is very low in case of fishnet units, which are owned by its owners.

In order to examine the relationship among the variables type of ownership of the fishnet units and the growth achieved. Chi- square test was applied. For applying Chi-square test, the following null hypothesis is fixed.

H_o : There is no significant difference in the growth among owned units, hired units and leased units in Kanyakumari district.

The alternative hypothesis is:

H_a : There is significant difference in the growth among owned units, hired units and leased units in Kanyakumari district.

The findings of the Chi- square test are presented in Table 4.12.

Table 4.12: Relationship Between the Type of Ownership and Growth-Chi-Square Test

Relationship	O	E	O - E	$(O - E)^2$	$(O - E)^{2/E}$
$R_1 C_1$	26	26.90	-.90	0.81	0.03
$R_1 C_2$	8	6.21	1.79	3.20	0.52
$R_1 C_3$	2	2.90	-0.90	0.81	0.28
$R_2 C_1$	39	38.10	.0.90	0.81	0.02
$R_2 C_2$	7	8.79	-1.79	3.20	0.36
$R_2 C_3$	5	4.10	0.90	0.81	0.20
Calculated Value					**1.41**

Source: Primary data.

df = 2

Table value at 5% level is 5.991.

Since the calculated value is less (1.41) than the Table value (5.991), the null hypothesis is accepted. Hence, it is concluded that there is no significant difference in growth among entrepreneurs owing business in different pattern. It implies that type of ownership is not a major variable having influence on the growth of fishnet units.

FORMS OF ORGANISATION

Industrial units fall under different forms of organisation. Sole proprietorship, partnership, co-operative and joint stock company are the most common forms of organisation.

The ownership pattern of small scale industry in India shows that about 87 per cent of the industrial units are in the form of soleproprietorship, 11.5 per cent is partnership and others are either co-operatives or joint stock company[1]. Each form of organisation has its merits and demerits. Similarly, each form of organisation is suitable for a particular case.

The businesses that require personal attention of the owners are generally organised as proprietary concerns. Similarly, the business providing direct services such as retailing, tailoring, hotels, bakery and the like are organised as soletrader concerns. Businesses requiring pooling of funds are started as partnership firms and the businesses which require huge investment are set up as joint stock companies.

1 Gordon, E., Natrajan, K., **Entrepreneurship Development,** Himalaya Publishing House, 2007, p. 81.

Further if the area of operation is wide, company form is appropriate whereas the proprietorship is suitable to the cases where the area of operation is confined to a particular locality. The willingness and capability to bear the business risk are other important considerations. If an entrepreneur is prepared to bear the risk he/she can set up the business as a proprietary concern or a partnership form. Otherwise, it is better to start as a company where the liability is limited. Business started for a specific duration on a temporary basis can be organised as proprietary or partnership concerns as it is easy to start and dissolve.

Of all the considerations, the choice of organisations depends basically on the nature of industrial activity proposed to be undertaken, the scale of operation, the scope of market to be covered and the sharing of risk.

The type of establishment or ownership pattern of fishnet units in Kanyakumari district shows that entrepreneurs have started fishnet units in all forms namely proprietorship, partnership and Joint Stock Company. The details are furnished in Table 4.13.

Table 4.13: Classification of Fishnet Units by Forms of Organisation

Sl. No.	Forms	Number of Units	Percentage
1.	Sole proprietorship	63	72.41
2.	Partnership	16	18.39
3.	Private limited company	8	9.20
	Total	**87**	**100.00**

Source: Primary data.

The Table 4.13 shows that out of 87 fishnet units, 63 units (72.41%) have been started as sole proprietorship units and 16 fishnet units (18.39%) have been started as partnership firms. Only a few fishnet units (9.20%) in Kanyakumari district have been started as private limited companies. This endorses the fact that most of the units in fishnet industry are small and medium scale enterprises.

It is observed that the growth achieved by the fishnet units and the forms of organisation have a direct relationship. Therefore a two-way table representing the relationship between the forms of organisation in the fishnet units and the growth achieved by them is prepared and presented in Table 4.14.

Table 4.14: Forms of Organisation and Growth Status of Fishnet Units

Forms	Status of Growth				Total	
	Growth		Non-Growth			
	No. of Units	Percentage	No. of Units	Percentage	No. of Units	Percentage
Sole proprietorship	29	46.03	34	53.97	63	100
Partnership	4	25.00	12	75.00	16	100
Private Limited Company	3	37.50	5	62.50	8	100
Total	**36**		**51**		**87**	**100**

Source: Primary data.

The Table 4.14 exhibits the growth and non growth of fishnet units in Kanyakumari district based on the forms of orgasnisation. It is observed that out of the total 63 fishnet units formed as soleproprietorship enterprises, 34 units (53.97%) are found to be non-growth units and 29 units (46.03%) have recorded growth. Among the 16 fishnet units formed as partnership firms, 12 fishnet units have recorded no growth and 25 per cent (4 fishnet units) have recorded growth. Further analysis finds that among the 8 fishnet units established as private limited companies, 3 fishnet units have recorded growth while and the remaining 5 fishnet units (62.5%) have not recorded any growth.

Thus, it is concluded that the growth is higher in case of soleproprietorship enterprises compared to the other forms of enterprises such as partnership and private limited companies.

In order to examine the relationship between the variables form of ownership of fishnet units and the growth status of fishnet units, Chi-square test is applied. For applying Chi-square test the following null hypothesis is fixed.

H_o : There is no significant difference in the growth of fishnet units among the fishnet units established under different forms of ownership.

The alternative hypothesis is

H_a : There is significant difference in the growth of fishnet units among the fishnet units established under different forms of ownership.

The finding of Chi-square test is presented in Table 4.15.

Table 4.15: Relationship Between Forms of Organisation and Growth-Chi-square Test

Relationship	O	E	(O - E)	$(O-E)^2$	$(O-E)^2/E$
$R_1 C_1$	29	26.07	2.93	8.58	0.38
$R_1 C_2$	4	6.62	-2.62	6.86	1.04
$R_1 C_3$	3	3.31	-0.31	0.10	0.03
$R_2 C_1$	34	36.93	-2.93	8.58	0.23
$R_2 C_2$	12	9.38	2.62	6.86	0.73
$R_2 C_3$	5	4.69	0.31	0.10	0.02
Calculated Value					2.38

Source: Primary data.

df = 2

The value at 5% level is 5.991.

Since the calculated value is less (2.38) than the table value (5.991), the null hypothesis is accepted. Hence, it is concluded that there is no significant difference in the growth achieved by the fishnet units established under different forms of organisation. It implies that a form of organisation is not a major variable having influence on the growth of fishnet units.

PERIOD OF ESTABLISHMENT

From time immemorial, in India fishnet has been manufactured manually by hand. Only in 1975 fishnet making was mechanised. Till 1990 no fishnet unit, was started in Kanyakumari district to manufacture fishnets. In 1990, hardly a few fishnet units came up. During this period there was no competition to the existing fishnet units so the selling price for fishnet was fixed by the manufactures at a high margin. Those who started fishnet units during this period earned a large amount of profit. But in course of time, many more units came in and now there is a competition among fishnet units to capture the market, so the profit has considerably reduced. Those who started before 2000 AD, earned a good profit and have shown a high growth in their business while those who started after 2000 AD are not able to show better growth as the former. Hence, the period of establishment of fishnet units has a relationship with the growth of fishnet units. Table 4.16 reveals the period of establishment of fishnet units in Kanyakumari district.

The Table 4.16 exhibits that out of 87 fishnet units, 59 fishnet units (67.82%) in Kanyakumari district were established during the period of 1995 to 2000 and another 14 fishnet units (16.09%) were established during the period of 1990 to 1995. The remaining 3.45 per cent of the fishnet units (3 units) were established during the period of 2005 to 2007. Thus, it shows a declining trend in establishment of new units in recent periods after 2000.

Table 4.16: Period of Establishment of Fishnet Units

Sl. No.	Year of Establishment	Number of Units	Percentages
1.	1990-1995	14	16.09
2.	1995-2000	59	67.82
3.	2000-2005	11	12.64
4.	2005-2007	3	3.45
	Total	**87**	**100.00**

Source: Primary data.

It is observed that the growth achieved by the fishnet units and the period of establishment have a direct relationship. Therefore, a two way table representing the relationship between the period of establishment and the growth achieved by them is prepared which is presented in Table 4.17.

Table 4.17: Fishnet Units by Period of Establishment

Period	Status of Growth				Total	
	Growth		Non-Growth			
	No. of Units	Percentage	No. of Units	Percentage	No. of Units	Percentage
Before 2000 AD	34	46.58	39	53.42	73	100
After 2000 AD	2	14.29	12	85.71	14	100
Total	**36**		**51**		**87**	**100**

Source: Primary data.

The Table 4.17 classified the fishnet units in Kanyakumari district into growth and non-growth units based on the period of establishment by the entrepreneurs. It is observed that among the 73 fishnet units established before 2000 AD, 34 fishnet units have registered growth (46.58%) and the remaining 39 fishnet units (53.42%) have shown no growth. Further analysis shows that among the 14 fishnet units established after 2000 AD, 12 fishnet units (85.71%) have recorded no growth and only two fishnet units (14.29%) have shown growth. It is concluded that growth is high among the units established earlier as compared to those established recently.

In order to examine the relationship between the variable period of establishment of the fishnet units and the growth status in the fishnet units, Chi-square test is applied. For applying Chi-square test, the following null hypothesis is fixed.

H_o : There is no significant difference in the growth of fishnet units among the fishnet units established during different periods.

The alternative hypothesis is

H_a : There is significant difference in the growth of fishnet units among the fishnet units established during different periods.

The findings of the Chi-square test are presented in Table 4.18.

Table 4.18: Relationship Between Period of Establishment and Growth-Chi-square Test

Relationship	O	E	O-E	$(O-E)^2$	$(O-E)^{2/E}$
R_1C_1	34	30.21	3.79	14.36	0.48
R_1C_2	7	5.79	-3.79	14.36	2.48
R_2C_1	39	42.79	-3.79	14.36	0.34
R_2C_2	12	8.21	3.79	14.36	1.75
Calculated Value					**5.05**

df = 1

Table value at 5% level is 3.84.

Since the calculated value is higher (5.05) than the table value (3.84), the null hypothesis is rejected and the alternative hypothesis is accepted. Hence, it is concluded that there is a significant difference in growth of fishnet units among the units established during different periods. It implies that period of establishment is a major variable which has a relationship with the growth of fishnet units.

NUMBER OF MACHINERIES USED

Fishnet industry is a capital intensive one. The major investment made in the industry is in machineries. Each of the machinery either yarn making one or net making one, costs more than nine lakh rupees whereas, if the same machinery is to be imported the cost runs to rupees 40 lakhs. Imported machinery is more efficient than the inland machinery. The quality of the end product manufactured by imported machinery is comparatively better than the products manufactured by the Indian machinery. Hence, in the market the products manufactured by the imported machinery are demanded more. This prompts the entrepreneurs to install foreign machineries in their industry. Each machinery has a specified capacity of production. While adding more and more machineries the entrepreneurs are able to increase their production and sales. This makes them grow better. Those entrepreneurs with limited number of machinery are not able to show better growth as the other entrepreneurs with more number of machineries. Hence, the number of machineries owned by an entrepreneur has relationship with the growth of fishnet units. Table 4.19 shows the details of machineries owned by the entrepreneurs of fishnet units in Kanyakumari district.

Table 4.19: Number of Machineries Used in Fishnet Units

Sl. No.	Number of Machineries	Number of Units	Percentage
1.	1 - 3	36	41.38
2.	3 - 6	15	17.24
3.	6 - 10	20	22.99
4.	10 - 15	10	11.49
5.	More than 15	6	6.90
	Total	87	100.00

Source: Primary data.

The Table 4.19 reveals that 36 fishnet units out of 87 fishnet units studied (41.38%) in Kanyakumari district have one to three machineries. Another set of 20 (22.99%) fishnet units have 6 to 10 machineries for their production and 15 fishnet units have 3 to 6 machineries. A very few fishnet units (6 units) are having more than 15 machineries for their production.

Thus, in most of the cases the number of machineries used ranged between 1 to 10. This implies that most of the fishnet units in Kanyakumari district are either small scale or medium scale units in terms of machineries.

Since it is observed that the growth achieved by the fishnet units and the number of machineries used by the entrepreneurs have a direct relationship, a two way table representing the relationship between the number of machineries used and the growth achieved by the entrepreneurs is prepared and presented in table 4.20.

Table 4.20: Number of Machineries Used by Entrepreneurs and Growth of Fishnet Units

Number of Machineries	Status of Growth				Total	
	Growth		Non-Growth			
	No. of Units	Percentage	No. of Units	Percentage	No. of Units	Percentage
Up to 6	20	39.22	31	60.78	51	100
More than 6	16	44.44	20	55.56	36	100
Total	**36**	–	**51**	–	**87**	**100**

Source: Primary data.

The inference of the two way table 4.20 is that out of 51 fishnet units with less than 6 machineries, 31 fishnet units (60.78 per cent) have shown no growth and the remaining 39.22 per cent (20 fishnet units) have shown growth. Further analysis reveals that out of the 36 fishnet units with more than 6 machines, 20 fishnet units (55.56%) have shown no growth and another 16 fishnet units (44.44%) have recorded growth.

Thus the growth is found comparatively higher among the fishnet units with more number of machineries than the units with less number of machineries. In order to observe the relationship between the variables number of machineries used by the entrepreneurs and the growth achieved by their units, Chi-square test is applied. For applying Chi-square test the following null hypothesis is fixed.

H_o : There is no significant difference in the growth among fishnet units having differing number of machineries.

The alternative hypothesis is

H_a : There is significant difference in the growth among fishnet units having differing number of machineries.

The finding of the Chi-square test is presented in Table 4.21.

Table 4.21: Relationship Between Number of Machinery Used and Growth-Chi-square Test

Relationship	O	E	O-E	$(O-E)^2$	$(O-E)^{2/E}$
R_1C_1	20	21.10	-1.10	1.21	0.06
R_1C_2	16	14.90	1.10	1.21	0.06
R_2C_1	31	29.90	1.10	1.21	0.04
R_2C_2	20	21.10	-1.10	1.21	0.06
Calculated Value					0.24

d.f = 1

Table value at 5% level is 3.84.

Since the calculated value is lower (0.24) than the table value (3.84), the null hypothesis is accepted. Hence, it is concluded that there is no significant difference in the growth achieved by entrepreneurs having less number of machineries and more number of machineries in the fishnet units. It implies that the number of machineries used is not a major variable in determining the growth.

VARIETY OF PRODUCTS MANUFACTURED

There are three categories of fishnets manufactured by different fishnet units. The first category of units produces nylon yarn which is the base for fishnet making. Units producing nylon yarn purchase nylon chips from Mumbai, Kolkata and Delhi and use it as a raw- material. Nylon yarn is technically referred to as nylon filament. Nylon yarn is the raw-material for the subsequent industrial units making fishnets. A group of entrepreneurs in the study area produce only nylon yarn. They do not engage in the subsequent processes.

Another group of fishnet units uses a mono (single) yarn or filament as raw-material and produce fishnet with either single knot or double knot. These fishnets are used for catching a particular category of fish. Similarly, another group of fishnet units use multi yarn or multi filaments as raw-material and produce either single knot or double knot fishnet. Each variety of fishnet is used for catching a particular category of fish.

In course of time many entrepreneurs who have started their units for manufacturing fishing yarn have started units manufacturing fishnet. Similarly, many other entrepreneurs who started their career with net making added yarn making in their business. Thus, as soon as the entrepreneur adds the new variety of product, he/she is able to show growth. So the variety of products manufactured by the entrepreneurs has a relationship with the growth achieved by them. Table 4.22 depicts the variety of products manufactured by entrepreneurs in Kanyakumari district.

Table 4.22: Variety of Fishnet Products Manufactured

Sl. No.	Type	Number of Units	Percentage
1.	Mono-Single Knot	38	43.68
2.	Mono-Double Knot	13	14.94
3.	Multi-Single Knot	9	10.34
4.	Multi-Double Knot	14	16.09
5.	Monofilament Yarn	8	9.20
6.	Multifilament Yarn	5	5.75
	Total	**87**	**100.00**

Source: Primary data.

Table 4.22 showing the variety of fishnet products manufactured reveals that out of 87 fishnet units in Kanyakumarii district, 38 fishnet units (43.68 per cent) have produced only monofilament single knot fishnets. Further analysis shows that 14 fishnet units (16.09 per cent) have manufactured multifilament double knot fishnets and another 8 fishnet units (9.20 per cent) have manufactured monofilament yarn in the study area. A few other units (9 fishnet units) have manufactured multifilament single knot fishnets and the remaining 5 fishnet units have produced multifilament yarn only.

Thus, it is clear that in Kanyakumari district most of the fishnet units are producing monofilament single knot fishnet. Next to that either monofilament double knot or multifilament double knot nets are produced in large number. Yarns are produced by a few units only.

Since it is observed that the growth achieved by the fishnet units and the variety of fishnet products manufactured by the fishnet units have a direct relationship, a two way table representing the relationship between the variety of products manufactured by the entrepreneurs and the growth achieved by them is prepared and presented in Table 4.23.

Table 4.23: Variety of Products Produced by the Entrepreneurs and Growth

Variety of Product	Status of Growth				Total	
	Growth		Non-Growth			
	No. of Units	Percentage	No. of Units	Percentage	No. of Units	Percentage
Product from monofilament	26	50.98	25	49.02	51	100
Product from multifilament	7	30.43	16	69.57	23	100
Yarn product	3	23.08	10	76.92	13	100
Total	**36**		**51**		**87**	**100**

Source: Primary data.

The Table 4.23 exhibits that 26 units out of 51 fishnet units producing monofilament fishnets have grown well while 25 fishnet units representing 49.02 per cent have miserably failed down to achieve growth. Among the 23 fishnet units producing multifilament fishnets, 7 fishnet units have recorded growth and 16 fishnet units have not registered any growth. Out of 13 fishnet units which are producing yarns only, 3 fishnet (23.08%) have registered growth while the remaining 10 fishnet units (76.92%) have not achieved any growth.

Thus, it is observed that the growth is high among the units producing monofilament products compared to other categories of products and it is very low among the units producing yarn products.

In order to examine the relationship between the variables, variety of products manufactured by the entrepreneurs and the growth in their fishnet units, Chi-square test is applied. For applying Chi-square test the following null hypothesis is fixed.

H_o : There is no significant difference in the growth among fishnet units producing different varieties of products.

The alternative hypothesis is:

H_a : There is significant difference in the growth among fishnet units producing different varieties of products.

The finding of the Chi-square test is presented in Table 4.24.

Table 4.24: Relationship Between Variety of Product Manufactured and Growth-Chi-square Test

Relationship	O	E	O - E	(O - E)^2	(o - E)$^{2/E}$
$R_1 C_1$	26	21.10	4.90	24.01	1.14
$R_1 C_2$	7	9.52	-2.52	6.35	0.67
$R_1 C_3$	3	5.38	-2.38	5.66	1.05
$R_2 C_1$	25	29.90	-4.90	24.01	0.80
$R_2 C_2$	16	13.48	2.52	6.35	0.47
$R_2 C_3$	10	7.62	2.38	5.66	0.74
Calculated Value					**4.87**

Source: Primary data.

df = 2

Table value at 5% level 5.991.

Since the calculated value is less (4.87) than the table value (5.991), the null hypothesis is accepted. Hence, it is concluded that there is no significant difference in growth achieved by entrepreneurs producing different varieties of products manufactured in the fishnet industry. Thus, it shows that the variety of products manufactured by the entrepreneurs is not a major variable which has a relationship with growth.

CAPITAL CONTRIBUTED BY THE OWNER (OWNED CAPITAL)

Starting of business especially when it is capital intensive requires heavy amount of capital from the entrepreneur. Capital is required for acquiring fixed assets like land, buildings, plant and machinery. Similarly, capital is required to meet the running expenditure also. Entrepreneurs with sound financial backing meet their requirements from their own funds. They are able to run their business successfully without any difficulty. Others who do not have sufficient finance mobilise it from friends and relatives. A few other entrepreneurs borrow it from banks and financial institutions. The entrepreneurs who borrow from banks and financial institutions pay heavy interest and find it hard to repay the loan. Such entrepreneurs with heavy loan obligation find it hard to grow in their business. Hence, the growth of fishnet units is related to the debt obligations of the entrepreneurs. Thus, there exists a relationship between the owned capital invested by the entrepreneur and the growth achieved by them. Table 4.25 furnishes the details of owned capital committed by the entrepreneurs in fishnet units in Kanyakumari district.

Table 4.25: Owned Capital Invested by Entrepreneurs and Growth in Fishnet Units

Sl. No.	Owned Capital	Number of Units	Percentage
1.	0 to 10 lakhs	4	4.60
2.	10 to 20 lakhs	38	43.68
3.	20 to 30 lakhs	20	22.99
4.	30 to 40 lakhs	14	16.09
5.	40 to 50 lakhs	11	12.64
	Total	**87**	**100.00**

Source: Primary data.

Table 4.25 showing the owned capital invested by the fishnet unit entrepreneurs reveals that 38 units out of 87 fishnet units (43.68%) in Kanyakumari district have invested their own capital which ranges between Rs. 10 to 20 lakhs. Further, 20 fishnet units (22.99%) have capital investment ranging between Rs. 20 and 30 lakhs. Another 14 fishnet units have the owned capital of Rs.30 to 40 lakhs and 11 fishnet units have the owned capital of Rs. 40 to 50 lakhs. The remaining four fishnet units (4.60%) have owned capital which is less than Rs. 10 lakhs.

Thus, in Kanyakumari district most of the fishnet units have invested between Rs. 10 lakhs and Rs. 40 lakhs as owned capital. Among them, in most of the cases it ranges between Rs.10 lakhs to 20 lakhs only. Only in case of 12.64 per cent of the units the amount of owned capital ranges between Rs. 40 and 50 lakhs.

Since it is observed that the growth achieved by the fishnet units and the owned capital invested by the entrepreneurs have a direct relationship, a two way table representing the relationship between the owned capital invested by the entrepreneurs and growth achieved by them is prepared and presented in Table 4.26.

Table 4.26 depicts that out of the 42 fishnet units having owned capital up to Rs. 20 lakhs in Kanyakumari district, 24 fishnet units (57.14%) have scored growth and 18 fishnet units have not recorded any growth. Further, the analysis reveals that out of 45 fishnet units having owned capital above Rs. 20 lakhs, 33 fishnet units (73.34%) have registered no growth and only 12 fishnet units (22.66%) have achieved growth.

Table 4.26: Owned Capital Invested by Entrepreneurs and Growth

Owned Capital	Status of Growth				Total	
	Growth		Non-Growth			
	No. of Units	Percentage	No. of Units	Percentage	No. of Units	Percentage
Up to 20 lakhs	24	57.14	18	42.86	42	100
Above 20 lakhs	12	26.66	33	73.34	45	100
Total	**36**		**51**		**87**	**100**

Source: Primary data.

Thus, it is observed that higher growth is registered among the fishnet units with lower amount of owned capital as compared to the units with higher amount of owned capital.

The relationship among the variables owned capital invested by the entrepreneurs and the growth in the fishnet units is examined with the help of Chi-square test. For applying Chi-square test the following null hypothesis is fixed.

H_o : There is no significant difference in the growth among fishnet units promoted by entrepreneurs with different sizes of owned capital.

The alternative hypothesis is:

H_a : There is significant difference in the growth among fishnet units promoted by entrepreneurs with different sizes of owned capital.

The finding of the Chi-square test is presented in Table 4.27.

Table 4.27: Relationship Between Capital Invested and Growth-Chi-square Test

Relationship	O	E	O - E	$(O - E)^2$	$(O - E)^{2/E}$
$R_1 C_1$	24	17.38	6.62	43.82	2.52
$R_1 C_2$	12	18.62	-6.62	43.82	2.35
$R_2 C_1$	18	24.62	-6.62	43.82	1.78
$R_2 C_2$	33	26.38	6.62	43.82	1.66
Calculated Value					**8.31**

Source: Primary data.

df = 1

Table value at 5% level is 3.84.

Since the calculated value is higher (8.31) than the table value (3.84), the null hypothesis is rejected and the alternative hypothesis is accepted. Hence, it is concluded that there is a significant difference in growth achieved by entrepreneurs with different sizes of owned capital. It implies that owned capital is a major variable which has a relationship with the growth of fishnet units.

NUMBER OF SHIFTS WORKED

In the capital intensive fishnet industry investment is heavy. More than 80 per cent of the total investment is made in machineries. Hence, entrepreneurs are reluctant to add more machinery. Instead they try to use the existing machineries to their fullest extent. When there is a heavy demand for fishnet, existing machinery is fully utilised for three shifts of 8 hours each. Working for three shifts without interruption requires the support of the employees. Further, an interrupted power supply and supply of raw-material assure three shift works. Any deficiency on the side of the entrepreneur with regard to the above interrupts production and curtails growth. Hence, the numbers of shifts worked in fishnet units and the growth achieved by them have a relationship. Table 4.28 depicts the details of shifts of work engaged in fishnet units in Kanyakumari district.

Table 4.28: Number of Shifts in Fishnet Units

Sl. No.	Number of Shifts	Number of Units	Percentage
1.	One	2	2.30
2.	Two	16	18.39
3.	Three	69	79.31
	Total	**87**	**100.00**

Source: Primary data.

Table 4.28 shows that among the total of 87 fishnet units in the study area, 69 fishnet units (79.31%) have been functioning with three shifts and 16 fishnet units have been functioning with two shifts and a negligible number of units (two) have been functioning with single shift system. Thus, it is clear that majority of the fishnet units in Kanyakumari district have been functioning under three shift system.

It is observed that the growth achieved by the fishnet units and the number of shifts worked in the units have a direct relationship. Therefore a two-way table representing the relationship between the number of shifts worked in the fishnet units and the growth achieved by them is presented in Table 4.29.

Table 4.29 shows the growth and non-growth units on the basis of number of shifts engaged by the entrepreneurs in fishnet industry in Kanyakumari district. It is clearly observed that out of the total 69 fishnet units working for three shifts 39 fishnet units have not achieved growth and 30 fishnet units (43.48 per cent) have achieved growth. Further, the analysis reveals that out of 16 fishnet units working with two shifts, 10 fishnet units (62.5 per cent) have recorded no growth and the remaining 6 fishnet units (37.5 per cent) have observed growth. Among the two fishnet units working for single shift, none have shown growth.

Table 4.29: Number of Shifts Worked and Growth Status of Fishnet Units

Shifts	Status of Growth				Total	
	Growth		Non-Growth			
	No. of Units	Percentage	No. of Units	Percentage	No. of Units	Percentage
One	0	–	2	100.00	2.00	100
Two	6	37.5	10	62.50	16.00	100
Three	30	43.48	39	56.52	69.00	100
Total	**36**		**51**		**87.00**	

Source: Primary data.

Thus, it can be concluded that the growth is comparatively higher in case of the fishnet units with more shifts than the units functioning with less number of shifts. In order to examine the relationship between the variables number of shifts worked in the fishnet units and the growth of the fishnet units, Chi-square test is applied. For applying chi-square test the following null hypothesis is fixed.

H_o : There is no significant difference in the growth of fishnet units among the fishnet units functioning with different number of shifts.

The alternative hypothesis is

H_a : There is significant difference in the growth of fishnet units among the fishnet units functioning with different number of shifts.

The finding of Chi-square test is presented in Table 4.30.

Table 4.30: Relationship Between Number of Shifts Worked and Growth-Chi-square Test

Relationship	O	E	O-E	$(O-E)^2$	$(O-E)^{2/E}$
R_1C_1	0	0.83	-0.83	0.69	0.83
R_1C_2	6	6.62	-0.62	0.38	0.06
R_1C_3	30	28.55	1.45	2.10	0.07
R_2C_1	2	1.17	0.83	0.69	0.59
R_2C_2	10	9.38	0.62	0.38	0.04
R_2C_3	39	40.45	-1.45	2.10	0.05
Calculated Value					1.64

Source: Primary data.

df = 2

Table value at 5% level is 5.991.

Since the calculated value is less (1.64) than the table value (5.991), the null hypothesis in accepted. Hence, it is concluded that there is no significant difference in growth among fishnet units with different number of shifts. It implies that number of shifts worked is not a major variable having influence on the growth of fishnet units.

SUMMARY

In this chapter ten entrepreneurial variables have been identified as having relationship with the growth of the fishnet units in Kanyakumari district. The relationship existing between these 10 variables and their growth has been exposed theoretically and explained through two-way tables. Subsequently, the relationships between the ten variables with the growth have been tested with the help of' Chi-square test. Statistical testing through 'Chi-square' test reveals that the following entrepreneurial variables have significantly influenced the growth of fishnet units in Kanyakumari district. They are:

(i) Community of the entrepreneur;

(ii) Owned capital invested; and

(iii) Period of establishment.

Further, it is identified that the following entrepreneurial variables do not influence the growth of fishnet units in Kanyakumari district.

(i) Ownership of business

(ii) Religion of entrepreneurs

(iii) Reason for starting the business

(iv) Variety of products manufactured

(v) Number of machineries used

(vi) Number of shifts worked

(vii) Forms of organisation

REFERENCES

1. John Kao and Howard Stevenson, *Entrepreneurship*, Division of Research, Harvard Business School, 1984, p. 34.
2. Gordon, E., Natrajan, K., *Entrepreneurship Development*, Himalaya Publishing House, Mumbai, Second Revised Edition, 2007, p. 1.
3. Say, J.B., *A Treatise on Political Economy*, Boston, 1924, Vol. 2, pp. 55-59.

4. Gupta, C.B., Srinivasan, N.P., *Entrepreneurial Development*, 2002, Sulthan Chand & Sons, New Delhi, p. 38.
5. *Op. cit.*, p. 2.
6. Schumpeter, J.A., *The Theory of Economic Development*, Cambridge Mass, Harvard University Press, 1959, p. 69.
7. *Ibid.*, p. 42.
8. *Ibid.*, p. 44.
9. *Op. cit.*, p. 2.
10. *Op. cit.*, p. 2.
11. Higgins, B., *The Economic Development*, The Free Press, Newyork, 1954, p. 219.
12. John Kao, *Entrepreneurship, Creativity and Organization*, Prentice Hall, New Jersey, 1989, p. 92.
13. William Diamond, *Development Banks*, The John Hiplines Press, Baltimore, 1957, p. 5.
14. Arthur H. Cole, *Business Enterprise in its Social Setting*, Cambridge, Harvard University Press, 1959, p. 44.
15. Joseph A. Schumpeter, *The Theory of Economic Development*, Harvard University Press, 1934, p. 48.
16. McClelland, *The Achieving Society*, D. Van Nostrand & Co., Newyork, 1961, pp. 210-215.
17. Gustar, F., Papanek, *The Development of Entrepreneurship*, The American Economic Review, 1962, pp. 46-58.
18. Kirzner, M., *Competition and Entrepreneurship*, University of Chicago Press, 1973, pp. 39-43.
19. Thomas Cochram, *The Entrepreneur in Economic Change*, Explorations in Entrepreneurial History, 1965, pp. 25-37.
20. Max Weber, *The Theory of Economic and Social Organization*, The Free Press, New York, 1978, p.7.
21. Bert, F. Hoselitz, *A Sociological Approach to Economic Development*, Development and Society, 1964, p. 24.
22. Everett E. Hagen, *The Economics of Development*, Vakil Feffer and Simmons Pvt. Ltd., Bombay, 1968, pp. 7-15.
23. Randall, G. Stokes, *The Afrikner Industrial Entrepreneur and Afrikner Nationalism*, Economic Development and Cultural Change, 1974, pp. 557-559.
24. Joseph, A. Schumpeter, *The Theory of Economic Development*, Harvard University Press, 1934, p. 68.
25. David C McCelland, *The Achieving Society*, The Free Press, New York, 1961, p. 256.

26. Hagen, E.E., *On the Theory of Social Change, How Economic Growth Begins,* Tavistock Publications, London, 1964, p. 169.

27. Kunkel, J.H., *Values and Behaviour in Economic Development,* Economic Development and Cultural Change, 1965, pp. 257-277.

28. Gordon, E., Natrajan, K., *Entrepreneurship Development,* Himalaya Publishing House, 2007, p. 81.

Factors Promoting Growth in Fishnet Industry

INTRODUCTION

Industrial growth is a common phenomenon that could be seen with both the newly started units and the existing ones. Industrial growth is the outcome of the influence of several factors. This chapter brings to light the factors causing growth of fishnet units in Kanyakumari district. The chapter begins with a theoretical background of the identified factors causing growth and ends with the level of influence of these factors on the growth of fishnet units.

Factor analysis has been employed to find out the level of influence of these factors on growth. Primary data collected from the fishnet industrial units with the help of a structured questionnaire have been used for the preparation of this chapter.

FACTOR ANALYSIS—AN INTRODUCTION

The personal observation of the researcher through personal visit to the field of study and the findings of the pilot study have been of much use in identifying the factors causing growth in fishnet units in Kanyakumari district. It has been identified that there are 21 variables responsible for the growth of fishnet units in Kanyakumari district.

FUNCTIONS OF FACTOR ANALYSIS

The factor analysis performs the following functions:

(i) Identifies the smallest number of common factors that best explain or account for the correlation among the indicators.

(ii) Identifies a set of dimensions that are latent (not easily observed) in a large number of variables.

(iii) Devises a method of combining or condensing a large number of variables with varying levels into distinctly different number of groups.

(iv) Identifies and creates an entirely new smaller set of variables to partially or completely replace the original set of variables for subsequent regression or discriminant analysis from a large number of variables. It is especially useful in multiple regression analysis when multicollinearity is focused to exist as the number of independent variables is reduced by using factors, and there by minimizing or avoiding multicollinearity. In fact, factors are used in lieu of original variables in the regression equation[1].

MATHEMATICAL FRAMEWORK

Factor analysis is a multi variate tool assisting the researcher, to reduce the innumerable variables into manageable number of factors. In factor analysis each variable is expressed as a liner combination of underlying factors. A factor is an underlying dimension that accounts for several observed variables. Factor loadings are those values which explain how closely the variables are related to each one of the factors discovered. Communality shows how much of each variable is accounted for by the underlying factor taken together. Rotation, in the context of factor analysis is some thing like staining a microscope slide. Just as different stains on it reveal different structures in the tissue, different stains on it reveal different structures in the data[2].

The amount of variance a variable shares with all other variables included in the analysis is referred to as communality. The co-variation among the variables is described in terms of a small number of common factors. These factors are not over observed.

The factor analysis model in matrix notation is given by

$$x = Af + e$$

where

$x = (x_1, x_2, x_3 \ldots x_p)$

$f = (f_1, f_2, f_3 \ldots fm)$

$e = (e_1, e_2, e_3 \ldots e_p)$

m = number of factors and

p = number of variables

and matrix

$$A = \begin{bmatrix} a_{11}, a_{12}, \ldots, \ldots, \ldots, a_{1m} \\ a_{21}, a_{22}, \ldots, \ldots, \ldots, a_{2m} \\ \ldots, \ldots, \ldots, \ldots, \ldots, \ldots, \\ a_{p1}, a_{p2}, \ldots, \ldots, \ldots, a_{pm} \end{bmatrix}$$

Where *aij* is factor loadings which give net correlation between the variables *xi* and factor *fj* (where $i = 1, 2, \ldots p$) and $j = 1, 2, 3 \ldots m$). It is assumed that the error variable *(e)* are distributed independently of *f* and *p* and *e* as multi-variate normal distribution.

One of the problems in dealing with the growth of fishnet industrial units is the wide number of variables to be taken into account for analysis. Factor analysis within broad limits of the computer can analyse the relationship between a large number of attributes or variables for many observations within a short spam of time.

Accordingly in the present study factor analysis is employed to reduce a set of 21 inter-dependent variables to a smaller set of more meaningful factors. It is hypothesised that growth of fishnet units *(y)* is due to socio-economic factors such as: *(i)* production factor; *(ii)* employee factor; *(iii)* background of the owner factor; *(iv)* marketing factor; and *(v)* competition factor. The detailed specifications of these variables are given separately in this chapter.

Factor analysis seems to be appropriate for this study, because of the problem of multi-collinearly which is quite common among various socio-economic variables in the fishnet industrial units. It would be very difficult to apply the commonly used regression techniques to the data regarding growth of fishnet industrial units as a dependent variable and socio-economic variables as independent variables.

ANALYTICAL FRAMEWORK

The principal factor analysis method is mathematically suitable for the solution to a factor problem. Its major solution features is the extraction of a maximum amount of variation as each factor is calculated[3]. Most of the analysis methods produce results in a form that is difficult or impossible to interpret. Thurston argued that it is necessary to rotate factor matrices to interpret them adequately[4]. He pointed out that original factor matrices are arbitrary in the sense that an infinite number or reference frames (axes) can be found to reproduce given 'R' matrix[5]. In order to move the axes from the arbitrary location determined by the methods of extraction to some portion useful for interpretation of the factors for comparison with other studies, the axes are rotated. A major goal of rotation is to obtain meaningful factor that are as consistent as possible from analysis to analysis[6]. There are several methods available for factor analysis. But the principal factor method is the widely used one. Further, orthogonal rotation maintain the independent factors that is, the angle between the axes are kept at 90 degrees. One of the final out comes of factor analysis is called rotated factor matrix, a table of co-efficient that expresses the ratios between the variables and the factors. The sum of the sequences of the factor loading of variables is called communalities *(h^2)*.

The communality of a factor is its common factor variance. The factor with factor loading of 0.50 or greater are considered as significant factors and the factors with less than 50 per cent common variation with the rotated factor pattern are too weak to report[7]. In the present study, the principal factor analysis method with Orthogonal Varimax Rotation is used to identify the significant set of influencing factors.

FACTORS PROMOTING GROWTH IN FISHNET UNITS

The factors influencing the entrepreneurs to start and/or manage fishnet units effectively and efficiently are innumerable in number. Even though the variables influencing growth are too many, the present study confines itself to 21 variables. The variables so identified for analysis are availability of raw materials, infrastructural facilities for production, uninterrupted power supply, availability of skilled manpower, previous experience in the industry, generation of ownership, localisation advantage, family support, type of competition, educational qualification, generation of ownership, communal settings, growth in capacity utilisation, external liabilities of the entrepreneurs, period of credit allowed, advertisement, export subsidy, expansion of marketing area of operation, usage of advanced machinery, assets background of the family and social status. The above said 21 variables have been identified to be promoting growth of fishnet units at varying levels.

AVAILABILITY OF RAW MATERIAL

One of the most important considerations involved in locating a fishnet unit at a particular locality is the availability of raw materials in the local area. The biggest advantage of availability of raw materials at the location of fishnet units is that it reduces the cost in terms of transportation. In case where the raw materials used are perishable, the consuming industrial units have to be necessarily located nearer to places where the raw materials are available. In fishnet units, the nylon yarn is used as the raw material. Even though the raw materials used in fishnet units are not of perishable nature, locating the units in the area where the raw materials are available in plenty gives many more added benefits[8].

Availability of raw material at the right time and adequate quantity is a key factor in determining the sustainability and growth of any industrial unit. In Kanyakumari district majority of the fishnet units depends on outside suppliers for raw materials. A few fishnet units alone manufacture nylon yarn to meet their own requirement, but it is not sufficient. Most of the fishnet units in Kanyakumari district get their raw materials from Coimbatore, Chennai, Pondicherry and other places outside Tamil Nadu. Table 5.1 clearly explains the place of consumption of raw materials by fish net units in Kanyakumari district.

Table 5.1: Area of Availability of Raw Materials

Sl. No.	Nature of availability	Number of units	Percentage
1.	Available in the local area	78	89.66
2.	Non-available in the local area	9	10.34
	Total	**87**	**100.00**

Source: Primary data.

The details of the availability of raw materials to the fishnet units in the study area are shown in Table 5.1. It is found that more than 89.66 per cent (78 units) of the fishnet units in the study area have purchased their raw materials from the local area as they are available without shortage in the area where their units are located. Remaining 10.34 per cent (that is 9 units) are affected by non- availability of raw materials in the local area. Those who do not have local supply of raw materials are worstly affected by the shortage of raw materials while there is high demand for fishnets in the market. These fishnet units fully depend on the suppliers from other areas. Hence, their production is affected at many times due to shortage of raw materials.

It is clear from analysis that majority of the fishnet units in Kanyakumari district enjoys the uninterrupted supply of raw materials. Hence production is smooth to them without any interruption throughout the year. However, it has seriously affected a group of fishnet units.

AVAILABILITY OF INFRASTRUCTURAL FACILITIES

Infrastructure plays a key role in the smooth functioning of an industrial unit. The infrastructural facilities required for an industry include transport, communication, power, water and banking. Availability of raw materials, finance and labour[9] become the other dominant factors promoting growth of fishnet units.

Infrastructural facilities are vital for the production in fishnet units. Infrastructural facilities needed for the production of fishnet units are proper machines, spacious building, proper ventilation, storage and water supply. Those fishnet units which do not have sufficient infrastructural facilities could not show growth as the units having sufficient infrastructural facilities. The details of availability of infrastructural facilities for fishnet units are shown in Table 5.2.

Table 5.2: Availability of Infrastructural Facilities

Sl. No.	Availability	Number of units	Percentage
1.	Available	76	87.36
2.	Not-Available	11	12.64
	Total	**87**	**100.00**

Source: Primary data.

Table 5.2 shows that 87.36 per cent of the fishnet units functioning in Kanyakumari district have sufficient infrastructural facilities needed for production. Only 11 units out of 87 units have no sufficient infrastructural facilities needed for their production.

UNINTERRUPTED POWER SUPPLY

A major bottle neck in the timely commencement and continuance of production is interrupted power supply. Interruption in power supply disrupts regularity of production. Further, the quality of the products finished is not up to the mark if the industrial unit has power interruption. Hence, interruption in power affects the marketability of the product. Therefore, majority of the fishnet units in Kanyakumari have erected their own power generating machineries to get rid of interruption in power supply. Installing generators in the fishnet unit requires heavy amount of capital investment. Further, the maintenance and running cost of the generator increases the cost of production of the fishnet unit. Hence, the growth of fishnet units is curtailed by interrupted power supply.

Interrupted power supply not only affects the production but also the quality of the finished product. The loss on account of inferior quality is high especially in the units where production is fully mechanised and automated. In order to increase production and high quality, most of the units have mechanised their production process. All such units which have mechanised their production process are seriously affected by the interruption in power supply. In Kanyakumari district, most of the fishnet manufacturing units depend on the Tamil Nadu Electricity Board (TNEB) for electricity. Only a few units have their own alternative arrangements for power supply. Hence, the growth of fishnet units is disturbed by interrupted power supply. Table 5.3 explains the interruption in power supply experienced by fishnet units in Kanyakumari district.

Table 5.3: Interruption in Production due to Interruption in Power Supply

Sl. No.	Status of Interruption	Number of units	Percentage
1.	Interrupted	73	83.91
2.	Uninterrupted	14	16.09
	Total	**87**	**100.00**

Source: Primary data.

It is clear from Table 5.3 that most of the fishnet units [83.91 per cent (73 units)] in the study area have the problem with regard to power supply. In other words, the production process of majority of the industrial units in Kanyakumari district is affected by interruption in power supply. Another 16.09 per cent of the total fishnet units alone are not disturbed by the shortage of power supply. These units have their own arrangement of generators to offset the problem of interruption in power supply.

AVAILABILITY OF SKILLED MANPOWER

Availability of skilled manpower is another factor promoting growth in fishnet units. Manpower is the back bone of any industrial process. Wherever there are machines and technology is involved there is a demand for manpower. As the technology goes in deep the need for skilled manpower familiar with the technology arises.

In those industries with high technology, skilled manpower is the basic requirement needed to run the industry. Such industrial units can not function in the absence of skilled manpower. Absence of skilled manpower can no more be substituted with other forms of labour. Attempting to employ unskilled labour in the place of skilled labour results in production of inferior quality of products. Hence, entrepreneurs especially in fishnet units prefer to employ only skilled manpower.

Since the entire production in fishnet units is mechanised, without skilled workers regular production cannot be carried out. Therefore, availability of skilled manpower has become a basic requirement for the growth of fishnet units.

It is significant to note that the fishnet units in Kanykumari district are highly affected by the shortage of trained and skilled workers. There is accute shortage of skilled manpower in the district. Table 5.4 clearly presents the availability of skilled manpower in fishnet units in Kanyakumari district.

Table 5.4 reveals that most of the fishnet units in Kanyakumari district are troubled with non-availability of skilled manpower that is 54 units out of

Table 5.4: Availability of Skilled Manpower

Sl. No.	Availability	Number of units	Percentage
1.	Sufficiently available	33	37.93
2.	Not-sufficiently available	54	62.07
	Total	**87**	**100.00**

Source: Primary data.

total 87 units representing 62.07 per cent in the district have reported as they are affected by shortage of skilled manpower. Another 33 fishnet manufacturing units out of 87 units studied in the study area are not affected by the short supply of skilled manpower. It is identified that those units which have reported that they have sufficient skilled manpower are bringing the skilled manpower required further from far off places by arranging their own transport. It increases the cost of production of the fishnet units.

The main reasons for non-availability of skilled manpower in the local area are the following. The wages offered in fishnet industry are not attractive as compared to other industries in the district. It ranges between Rs. 2000/- to Rs. 3000/- per month. This is not attractive to the labourers in Kanyakumari district. Hence, the skilled workers do not reside in the local district once when they are technically qualified.

Further, most of the female workers who are technically qualified do not continue their job after marriage. They resign their job on such occasion. Therefore, the labour turnover is high in this industry.

Another reason for the shortage of skilled manpower in Kanyakumari district is the absence of formal training for workers. Though Kanyakumari district has a sizable population, with high literacy rate, many of them are not technically qualified. Hence, there is always an acute shortage for skilled manpower in the district. Most of those who are employed for the first time learn and earn skills only by experience. Moreover, there is no guarantee that experienced workers will remain in the same unit. They fly away from one job to another as soon as they qualify in the job.

Similarly, the shift system what is practised in the fishnet unit is not acceptable and adaptable to skilled workers. Skilled workers in the district prefer to work only in the regular working hours. They do not prefer to go job in night shifts and other shifts which do not suit them.

As fishnet units in Kanyakumari district is featured with lack of adequate skilled manpower, switchover of workers from one unit to other units has become a common day to day affair in the industry. It seriously affects the growth of fishnet units in Kanyakumari district.

PREVIOUS EXPERIENCE IN THE FISHNET INDUSTRY

Experience is the knowledge gained by a worker through observation or actual doing, and personal knowledge. Experience generally refers to know-how or procedural knowledge to carry out products. A person with considerable experience in a certain field gains knowledge and become an expert in the field. Many of the employees who have been employed as employees in some undertaking have become entrepreneurs in due course. The experiences what do they gain out of past work in a job make him/her fully qualified and competent to start an industrial units. Similarly, many others who have born in the business family learn business from their forefathers and family members which make them qualified to start an industrial unit later.

In Kanyakumari district, one could notice that many of the present day employers of fishnet units were the erst while employees in similar units in the industry. So the experience what a worker gains from employment motivates him/her to start unit. It could also be seen in the study area that many of the entrepreneurs who were employees with similar fishnet units before they start this unit have become successful in starting and running the unit. On the contrary, many others who have started their fishnet units without experience have miserably failed and closed down their units because of their inexperience. This shows that previous experience of the entrepreneurs make the entrepreneur to lead a success and show a growth in business.

The details of previous experiences of the entrepreneurs in fishnet units in Kanyakumari district is presented in Table.5.5.

Table 5.5: Previous Experience of the Entrepreneurs

Sl. No.	State of Experience	Number of units	Percentage
1.	Experience in other business	21	24.14
2.	Experience in the same business	26	29.89
3.	Inexperienced	40	45.97
	Total	**87**	**100.00**

Source: Primary data.

Table 5.5 shows the state of previous experiences of the entrepreneurs who are running fishnet units in the study area. It reveals that 45.97 per cent of fishnet owners have started their industrial unit without any experience in the fishnet industry or in any other industry. Eventhough rest of them are found to have started the present fishnet units with previous experience, only 29.89 per cent (26 owners out of 87 units), have the business experience in the same industry as a partner, supervisor, electrician, and worker.

Another 21 fishnet unit owners representing 24.14 per cent of the total entrepreneurs have business experience in other industries. Eventhough their experience is not so specific to fishnet industry, their knowledge in other industry helped them to improve their administrative ability.

TYPE OF FORMATION

Starting a new unit is very difficult because getting clearance and permission from various departments related to the industry is not so simple. But those with previous experience start the unit easily without difficulty. The new entrants are not familiar with the procedures of starting an industrial unit. Hence, it took a long time for them to start a unit. Hence, there is a hesitation among entrepreneurs to start a new industrial undertaking. This has discouraged many entrepreneurs not to start new industrial units.

In order to avoid the problems related to formation of an industry many entrepreneurs outrightly purchase the well functioning units and own them. This make them free from the burden of complying with legal formalities. Such entrepreneurs who outrightly purchase industrial units smoothly run the undertaking without much difficulty.

Another way opted by entrepreneurs to establish a fishnet unit is inheriting the business unit owned by their forefathers. Those who start their carrier as assisting their forefathers in business have become the owners of the unit in due course. These types of entrepreneurs do not experience any problem in the administration of the unit.

Fishnet units in Kanyakumari district have been started in three forms. They are newly started ones, outrightly purchased one and the inherited units. Table 5.6 explains the type of formation of fishnet units in Kanyakumari district.

Table 5.6: Type of Formation of Fishnet Units

Sl. No.	Type of Formation	Number of units	Percentage
1.	New	63	72.41
2.	Inherited	9	10.34
3.	Outright purchase	15	17.25
	Total	**87**	**100.00**

Source: Primary data.

The table 5.6 evidently shows that many of the fishnet units in the study area are newly established ones. It is clear that 72.41 per cent of the total units surveyed in the study have been started by the entrepreneurs as fresh. Another 17.25 per cent of the units have been acquired by the owners on outright purchase basis from other entrepreneurs. Many of the existing entrepreneurs sell their fishnet units for many reasons. Those entrepreneurs who are unable to manage the business effectively sell it outright in the market. Similarly, those units which are in sickness for many reasons are also sold in the market. Financial difficulty, marketing difficulty, personal/family problems and poor profitability are some of the other reasons for which many fishnet units are either closed down or sold in the market. It is further clear that only 10.34 per cent of the units are inherited by the present entrepreneurs from their forefather. These units are run as family business units for generations together.

All these above mentioned facts imply that majority of the fishnet unit owners in Kanyakumari district are first generation businessmen and are lacking experience in the field.

LOCALISATION ADVANTAGE

Location is an important factor in the success of an industrial unit. It has a substantial effect upon the operations of the unit. Localisation of the industry means location of industrial units manufacturing similar products in a single area. There are many advantages due to industrial units located in an area where localisation spreads. There is a good chance for industrial units located in an area to exchange their goods and services within themselves. Similarly, the benefits of common tool room, common effluent treatment and the like could be availed if industrial units are located in a specified area. Generally the places where localisation of industrial units takes place are close to raw materials market and finished goods market. The facilities such as transportation, electricity, water supply and the like are sufficiently available in the places of localisation. The Government attempts to develop such industrial centres into industrial clusters. The units located in such identified area enjoy benefits like tax concessions, power subsidy, and sales tax deferment. Those units which are not started in the identified industrial clusters do not enjoy any concessions. Such units have to grow independently. Units functioning in non-localised areas find it hard to survive.

In Kanyakumari district fishnet units are functioning in large number at two places. One is around A.N. Kudy and another one is around Industrial Estate, Konam. More than 75 per cent of total fishnet units in the district function in these two centres. The other 25 per cent fishnet units alone are scattered throughout the district. Table 5.7 exhibits localisation of fishnet units in Kanyakumari district.

It is observed that most of the fishnet manufacturing units (30 units) in Kanyakumari district are concentrated around Konam Industrial Estate and A.N.Kudy, that is 32 units which are close to one another. It is peculiar to note that both of the two centres viz., Konam Industrial Estate and A.N.

Table 5.7: Area of Localisation of Fishnet Units

Sl. No.	Area	Number of units	Percentage
1.	Konam Industrial Estate	30	34.48
2.	A.N.Kudy	32	36.78
3.	Other Area	25	28.74
	Total	87	100.00

Source: Primary data.

Kudy are located within Nagercoil Municipality. Units located in these two centres enjoy the benefit of uninterrupted power supply, good transportation facilities and cheap labour supply. Rest of the 25 fishnet units studied are scattered over other places, such as Vellamody, Pudur, Manavalakurichy, Manikattipottal, Colachel and Senbagaramanputhur.

TYPE OF FAMILY SUPPORT

In the success of an industrial unit, the support of the family members is essential. The family members such as wife, sons, daughters, brothers, sisters and other relatives help their family members to run the business successfully. The units getting assistance from their family members enjoy success over the units which do not get any assistance from their family members.

Members of the family of the entrepreneurs assist the business as employee, manager, partner and financier. In some families, the support enjoyed by entrepreneurs is overwhelming and such businesses succeed better than the units which do not command support from the family.

In Kanyakumari district most of the fishnet units get some type of support from their family members. Thus, the type of family support the entrepreneur enjoys has become a factor for analysis. Table 5.8 exhibits the type of family support the entrepreneurs of fishnet units in Kanyakumari district enjoy in running the business.

Table 5.8: Type of Family Support

Sl. No.	Type	Number of units	Percentage
1.	Employee	12	13.79
2.	Manager	20	22.99
3.	Partner	18	20.69
4.	Financier	11	12.64
5.	No support	26	29.89
	Total	87	100.00

Source: Primary data.

It is significant to note through Table 5.8 that nearly two- third (70.11%) of the owners of the fishnet manufacturing units in Kanyakumari district are supported by their family members. The family members support the owners as partners, financiers, managers, employees and so on. However, it is observed in the study the support enjoyed by entrepreneurs from their family members is in the form of assistance in management and day to day operations. Around one-third of the owners of fishnet units in Kanyakumari district have received support from their family members in the form of finance. It is further identified that 20.69 per cent of the family members of the entrepreneurs have extended their support as partners and 12.64 per cent of the entrepreneurs have got the support from their family members as financier. On analysis, it is found that 29.89 per cent of the total respondents did not receive any support from their family members. It is clear that they have started their fishnet units based on their own knowledge and experience.

TYPE OF COMPETITION

Competition plays a crucial role in the growth of any industry. Unhealthy competition in the industry leads to stagnation and failure of many units. Even within an industrial segment, different industrial units face different types of competition. Normally an industry faces any of the following forms of competition such as price, quality of product and brand image. On the other side, competition adds strength to the undertaking facing competition. An industrial unit facing stiff competition from the competitors makes it well equipped to face the competition. Such industrial units make themselves able to face the competition. So, though competition in a market in a sense limits industrial activity, it becomes a motivating force for growth.

In Kanyakumari district, the fishnet units face four types of competition namely price competition, quality competition, brand image competition and price and quality competition. There are few units, who have reported that they do not face any competition in the market. Absence of competition in the market makes them lazy. They are not active. They do not show better growth. The other units facing price competition compete with their competitors in price. They quite often change the price and compete with their competitors. Frequent change in price reduces profit. The growth of such fishnet units is moderate. There are many other units who face quality competition and brand competition. These units which fight to build brand image fight rigorously with other units in the market. Another group of fishnet units facing price and quality competition fight very hard to capture the market. Since, the competition faced by this type of units are twinfold, fishnet units facing this type of competition find it very hard to succeed. Hence, the type of competition faced by the fishnet units has become a factor promoting growth. Table 5.9 shows the type of competition faced by fishnet units in Kanyakumari district.

Table 5.9: Types of Competition

Sl. No.	Type	Number of units	Percentage
1.	Price competition	48	55.17
2.	Quality competition	24	27.58
3.	Brand image competition	4	4.60
4.	Price and quality competition	8	9.20
5.	No competition	3	3.45
	Total	**87**	**100.00**

Source: Primary data.

It is very significant to note from Table 5.9 that only 3 units out of 87 units studied have no competition. It is noteworthy to mention that 55.17 per cent of the total fishnet units in Kanyakumari district are experiencing price competition. Next to price, quality of the product is the most important competitive factor. Quality of the product has become a factor of competition to 27.58 per cent of the fishnet units. Only a few fishnet units (4.60%) have the brand image competition. It means brand image of other fishnet units is the least important competitive factor. Another factor with least significance (9.20%) is price and quality competition.

EDUCATIONAL QUALIFICATION

Education enlarges one's thinking and understanding. Education is one of the important factors needed to run an enterprise successfully. Educational qualification enriches the personality of the entrepreneurs. Entrepreneurial qualities and managerial abilities are often associated with the educational qualification of the people. Educated entrepreneurs have a wider knowledge on effective management. Those who have no education or little education could not so effectively administer their businesses as the educated entrepreneurs. Hence, the industrial units managed by educated entrepreneurs show better growth than others managed by uneducated entrepreneurs. There is a positive relationship between educational qualification possessed by the entrepreneurs and the growth recorded by the industrial units managed by them.

Kanyakumari is one of the highly educated districts in Tamil Nadu. The district has many numbers of educated entrepreneurs. Many of the educated entrepreneurs are professionally qualified in their field. Professionally qualified entrepreneurs administer their units well and facilitate growth.

Table 5.10 shows the educational qualifications of the owners of fishnet units in Kanyakumari district.

Table 5.10: Educational Qualification of Entrepreneurs

Sl. No.	Educational Qualification	Number of units	Percentage
1.	Professional	8	9.20
2.	Post graduate	11	12.64
3.	Graduate	28	32.18
4.	Diploma	11	12.64
5.	HSC	10	11.49
6.	SSLC	19	21.85
	Total	**87**	**100.00**

Source: Primary data.

It is very significant to note through Table 5.10 that there are no illiterate entrepreneurs in fishnet industry in Kanyakumari district. More than half of the entrepreneurs (47 fishnet units) which represent 54.02 per cent in the fishnet units are either graduates, post-graduates or professionals. Another 12.64 per cent are diploma holders and 11.49 per cent have had the higher secondary qualification. Entrepreneurs with SSLC as their educational qualification are 19 in number (21.85%). The above categorisation reveals that the over all educational qualification of the entrepreneurs in fishnet industry in Kanyakumari district is good.

GENERATION OF OWNERSHIP

In India many of the industrial units are continuously carried on for years together. Being an on-going concern, a business unit will continue functioning even after the life-time of its entrepreneur. Even in the next generation, the successor of the entrepreneur continues the business. In the beginning, the wards of entrepreneurs assist their fathers in business. The ward learns to manage the business unit by sitting on the side of the entrepreneur in the business. On his/or her death or at the latter years the ward succeeds the entrepreneur and runs the business. The successor of the entrepreneur, otherwise referred to as second generation entrepreneur runs the unit more efficiently than his/or her predecessor. The lesson what the successor learnt from his/her predecessor is of immense use to him/her in administering the business unit. But in practice, there are many other entrepreneurs who have started the businesses a fresh. Either the experience they have got as employee from other businesses or the educational qualification or supports of family and friends or any other factor may have prompted such people to start an industrial unit on their own. Such first generation entrepreneurs find it hard in the initial years to succeed in their business. A few of such entrepreneurs failed in their businesses while a few others improved a few years later. Hence, the generation of ownership of the entrepreneurs has a close relationship with the growth of the industrial units run by him/her.

In Kanyakumari district fishnet units are owned and managed by first generation and second generation entrepreneurs. Table 5.11 exhibits the generation of ownership of entrepreneurs.

Table 5.11: Generation of Ownership in Fishnet Industry

Sl. No.	Type	Number of units	Percentage
1.	First Generation	78	89.66
2.	Second Generation	9	10.34
	Total	**87**	**100.00**

Source: Primary data.

Table 5.11 reveals that out of 87 fishnet units 89.66 per cent of the units are run by first generation entrepreneurs and another 10.34 per cent (9 fishnet units) of the industrial units are run by second generation entrepreneurs. It shows that in Kanyakumari district majority of the fishnet units are started and run by first generation entrepreneurs. The reason for this trend may be that Kanyakumari district mainly depends on agriculture. Most of the people in Kanyakumari district directly and indirectly engage in agriculture. Further, the district is industrially backward. So, most of the people have not started industries. Now only the younger generation has started a few industrial units. As the result most of the industrial units in Kanyakumari district are run by first generation entrepreneurs.

COMMUNITY ENTREPRENEURSHIP

Fishnet is a product used in fishing by fishermen as gears. Fishermen know well about the quality specifications and market potential of fishnet. Therefore, involvement of fishermen in fishnet is more. Many of the entrepreneurs hailing from fishermen community have started fishnet units to meet their community requirements. But now many fishnet units are run by entrepreneurs from other communities. Entrepreneurs belonging to non-fishermen community view fishnet manufacturing as a wonderful business yielding assured return every year.

In Kanyakumari district, fishnet units are managed both by fishermen and non-fishermen community entrepreneurs. Both of them are equally competitive. Table 5.12 clearly explains the details of community based entrepreneurship in fishnet industry in Kanyakumari district.

Table 5.12: Classification of Entrepreneurs by Community

Sl. No.	Community	Number of units	Percentage
1.	Fishermen	21	24.14
2.	Non-Fishermen	66	75.86
	Total	**87**	**100.00**

Source: Primary data.

It is observed that Table 5.12 reveals that a majority of the entrepreneurs in the fishnet manufacturing industry in Kanyakumari district belong to non-fishermen communities. Non-fishermen community entrepreneurs constitute 75.86 per cent of the total entrepreneurs of fishnet units in Kanyakumari district. Only 24.14 per cent of the entrepreneurs in the district belong to the fishermen communities. Thus, entrepreneurship from fishermen community in the industry is low when compared with non-fishermen communities.

CAPACITY UTILISATION

Maximum production that can be produced by an undertaking under the normal working condition represents the production capacity. All institutions cannot attain the highest production capacity under all occasions. A few concerns that have attained the highest production capacity in any one year are not being able to sustain it in the subsequent years. Hence, utilisation of capacity is not a constant one, which is always subject to variation. Capacity utilisation is an index of the efficiency of an industry. In order to increase the productivity, an undertaking the capacity of the industry has to be fully utilised. In order to utilise capacity to its maximum extent, the vital resources such as inventory, human resources, finance and the like have to be utilised to their fullest extent.

There are a number of reasons for under utilisation of capacity by a firm. They are:

(i) Over supply of fishnet in the market due to entry of competitors;

(ii) Fall in market demand due to changes in consumer tastes;

(iii) Marketing failures; and

(iv) Seasonal reduction in demand.

In fishnet industry, shortage of skilled labour and frequent interruption in power supply are the two main factors which limit the utilisation of full capacity. The details of capacity utilisation by fishnet units in Kanyakumari district are presented in Table 5.13.

Table 5.13: Capacity Utilisation in Fishnet Industry

Sl. No.	Growth in capacity (Compound Growth Rate) (%)	Number of units	Percentage
1.	Below 0	2	2.30
2.	0 to 5	38	43.68
3.	5 to 10	45	51.72
4.	10 to 15	2	2.30
	Total	**87**	**100.00**

Source: Primary data.

Table 5.13 explains that out of the 87 fishnet units functioning in Kanyakumari district, 45 units representing 51.72 per cent have recorded a positive compound growth ranging between five and 10 per cent in terms of capacity utilisation in the last 10 years. Another 38 units (43.68%) have growth of zero to 5 per cent in terms of capacity utilisation. Only two units have the growth of 10 to 15 in terms of capacity utilisation in the past 10 years. Analysis of the growth of capacity utilisation in fishnet industry in Kanyakumari district reveals that 95 per cent of the total units functioning have shown a growth in capacity utilisation between zero to 10 per cent. It concludes that fishnet industry in the last 10 years have not grown well. The main reasons for the slow growth of fishnet units in Kanyakumari district are that the number of growing competitors and rising cost of raw-materials.

EXTERNAL LIABILITIES OF THE ENTREPRENEURS

Liabilities are the debts of an enterprise which arise out of borrowings from banks and other financial institutions. As long as an entrepreneur depends upon the institutional credit for his/her financial requirement, the financial cost of the unit is high. Hence, to the possible extent, the entrepreneurs try to clear their debts at the earliest. But, as long as the external debts are within their manageable limit, the institution will show good results. Hence, external liabilities of the enterprise become a variable contributing to growth in fishnet units. The growth/decline of external liabilities of the fishnet units are analysed with the help of the borrowed funds of the entrepreneurs. The institutions with higher growth rate of external liabilities fail to show overall growth in the institution. On the contrary, those institutions with lower external liabilities show better growth in real term. Hence the external liability has become a factor influencing the growth of fishnet units in Kanyakumari district.

Table 5.14 shows the details of external liabilities of the entrepreneurs of fishnet units in Kanyakumari district.

Table 5.14: External Liabilities of the Entrepreneurs

Sl. No.	External Liabilities	Number of units	Percentage
1.	Up to 25 Lakhs	16	18.39
2.	25 to 50 Lakhs	52	59.77
3.	50 to 75 Lakhs	14	16.09
4.	75 to 1 crore	5	5.75
	Total	**87**	**100.00**

Source: Primary data.

Table 5.14 exhibits the categorisation of fishnet units in Kanyakumari district, on the basis of the external liabilities of its entrepreneurs. It shows that a majority of the fishnet units (52 out of 87 fishnet units) in Kanyakumari district have external liabilities between Rs. 25 lakhs to 50 lakhs. Further analysis reveals that a very few fishnet units (5 units) alone have the external liabilities ranging between Rs. 75 lakhs to 1 crore. Another 16 fishnet units (18.39%) are having their external liabilities up to 25 lakhs only. Another group of 14 fishnet units (16.09%) have external liabilities ranging between Rs. 50 lakhs to Rs. 75 lakhs. The amounts of external liability vary according to their production capacity and the number of machineries used.

PERIOD OF CREDIT ALLOWED FOR RAW MATERIAL PURCHASE

Raw materials required for fishnet production are purchased from inland and foreign suppliers. Inland suppliers are located throughout the country. Small fishnet units and the fishnet units in the beginning stages do not have sufficient amount to invest in raw materials. Hence they depend upon credit from suppliers. A few suppliers are liberal in granting credit while a few others are conservative in granting credit. The suppliers who grant liberal credit add interest with the cost. Thus, the cost of purchase of raw materials for those who avail credit goes up. While the others who do not avail credit from suppliers, purchase raw materials for cash from their own funds.

In fishnet units in Kanyakumari district, the period of credit allowed varies from 7 days to 60 days. Table 5.15 clearly exhibits the period of credit allowed by the suppliers to their buyers in Kanyakumari district.

Table 5.15 exhibits that out of 87 fishnet units in Kanyakumari district, 13.79 per cent (12 units) are not at all allowed any credit for raw material purchase, 4.60 per cent (4 units) have availed credit up to 7 days. Another 31 fishnet units (ie. 35.63%) have availed 15 days credit, 27.59 per cent (24 units) of the total fishnet units have availed 30 days credit. It is further clear that 12.64 per cent (11 units) of the fishnet units have availed 45 days credit, 5.75 per cent (5 units) have availed 60 days period of credit allowed for raw- material purchase. It shows that in Kanyakumari district normally the fishnet units have availed credit which ranges up to 30 days.

Table 5.15: Period of Credit Allowed for Raw material Purchase

Sl. No.	Period Allowed	Number of units	Percentage
1.	No credit	12	13.79
2.	7 days	4	4.60
3.	15 days	31	35.63
4.	30 days	24	27.59
5.	45 days	11	12.64
6.	60 days	5	5.75
	Total	**87**	**100.00**

Source: Primary data.

ADVERTISING IN FISHNET UNITS

Advertisement in print and electronic media makes the product popular among consumers. The popular media of advertising are newspaper, magazine, journals, radio, television, posters, internet and the like. Though the advertisement is costly as it increases the sales and thus the profitability, every company spends on advertisements.

In fishnet units, eventhough advertisement is not a common phenomenon, a group of fishnet units advertise though online advertising in internet. Online advertising is the form of promotion that uses the internet and World Wide Web for the expressed purpose of delivering marketing messages to attract customers. The online advertisements made in internet make the availability of fishnet to all and it improves the image of the product.

Table 5.16: Advertising in Fishnet Units

Sl. No.	Advertisement status	Number of units	Percentage
1.	Advertising	7	8.05
2.	Non-Advertising	80	91.95
	Total	**87**	**100.00**

Source: Primary data.

Table 5.16 shows that out of 87 fishnet units, only 8.05 per cent (7 units) have involved in advertising their products and another 91.95 per cent (80 units) have not advertised their products. It shows that in Kanyakumari district majority of the fishnet units have not involved in advertising their products. The reasons may be that, entrepreneurs in Kanyakumari district are not ready to bear the advertisement cost or they have not realised the significance of advertisement.

EXPORT SUBSIDY

Export provides an opportunity to make the products available to foreign consumers. An export implies that local goods produced are sent to another country for sale. Export of goods requires involvement of the customs clearances in both the country of export and the country of import. Export brings new market and new customers to the company. Exporting company earns high profit out of increased turnover. Export of goods and services creates the product in the international market. It brings foreign exchange for the home country Foreign exchange is a good indicator of growth of the company and the national economy. Hence, every country directly and indirectly encourages the companies in the country to export more. One of the important means of promoting export is granting subsidy. The Government of India encourages 100 per cent Export Oriented Units in the country. This category of units is not allowed to do local sales. The export oriented fishnet manufacturing units in Kanyakumari are very small in number (3 units only). Another few fishnet units sell their products domestically as well as in international market. All the units which are exporting their products to foreign countries are eligible for export subsidy from the government.

Table 5.17: Export Subsidy Availed by Fishnet Units

Sl. No.	State of Subsidy	Number of units	Percentage
1.	Availed	7	8.05
2.	Not-Availed	80	91.95
	Total	**87**	**100.00**

Source: Primary data.

Table 5.17 reveals that out of 87 fishnet units, 8.05 per cent (7 units) have availed export subsidy and another 91.95 per cent (80 units) have not availed export subsidy. It clearly shows that a vast majority of the fishnet units in Kanyakumari district have not engaged in the export trade. The main reason for this is the lack of international standard in the quality of productior due to the non-availability of high quality machinery and well trained technicians and non application of high quality materials.

EXPANSION OF MARKETING AREA OF OPERATION

Expansion of market and increase in market share are the indicators of growth of many industrial enterprises. Expansion of market increases the sales volume of firms. In order to meet the increased demand, the scale of operation and production are increased. Expansion of market is represented through the increased coverage of market. An industrial unit covering national and international market shall be rated high in terms of its achievement than those units which confine their coverage to local and state level markets. Hence, every industry is resorting to cover a wide area. Many units which are started as small units in a local area grow bigger by widening its market. The units which try to reach the global market have to make their products qualitatively suitable to the international market specifications and internationally competitive. Thus, the increased coverage of market area indicates the growth of a business enterprise and the eagerness of the entrepreneurs to achieve high.

In case of the fishnet units in Kanyakumari district, most of the unit's market coverage is confined to the state level only. It is significant to note that 37.93 per cent of the fishnet units in the district cover the national level market and 8.04 per cent of the fishnet units market their products globally (Vide Table 5.18).

Table 5.18: Marketing Coverage of the Fishnet Units

Sl. No.	Market Coverage	Number of Units	Percentage
1.	Local only	8	9.20
2.	Local to state level	39	44.83
3.	Local to national level	33	37.93
4.	Local to international level	7	8.04
	Total	**87**	**100.00**

Source: Primary data.

Table 5.18 gives the classification of fishnet industrial units by their market coverage. It is significant to note that only 7 out of 87 fishnet units that are 8.04 per cent have their market at international level. A majority of the fishnet units have a market coverage at state level and national level which is clearly indicated by 44.83 per cent and 37.93 per cent respectively. Further, it states clearly only a few industrial units that are 8 fishnet units, out of 87 have restricted their activity the local market because of their low level of production and supply. Hence these types of industries are not competing with their quality at the state level and national level market operations.

TYPES OF MACHINERY

Adoption of latest technology is a criterion to assess the dynamism of an industrial unit. Growing entrepreneurs adapt to the latest technology. Employment of latest technology helps to increase the production and improve the quality of the manufacturing of product. Further, adôption of latest technology reduces the cost of production, sometimes the usage of advanced technology simplifies the manual work. Due to usage of advanced machinery, the number of employees required to carry out production is reduced and it minimises the cost. Similarly, many other benefits accrue to the entrepreneur by the adoption of advanced technology. Hence, adopting advanced technology is an indicator of growth of an industrial unit.

In fishnet units, there are two types of machinery used. One is the machinery made by the local companies and the other one is the machinery made by companies in the foreign countries. Foreign machineries are costly. Foreign machinery cost Rs. 40 lakhs to 70 lakhs while Indian machinery costs only Rs. 8 Lakhs to 14 lakhs. The production capacities of the machineries are different. Indian machinery is capable of producing 1000 Knots per hour. But the foreign machinery is capable of producing 1500 knots with perfection. Similarly, the quality of the fishnets manufactured by foreign machinery is also very high. In Kanyakumari district, during the initial period, very few of the fishnet units started their production with foreign machineries and in due course they started purchasing the local machineries. Now-a-days most of the fishnet industrial units in Kanyakumari district are using the Indian made machines. A few units use either foreign machine or Indian machines. Table 5.19 shows the details of types of machinery used in the fishnet units in the study area.

Table 5.19: Type of Machinery Used

Sl. No.	Type	Number of Units	Percentage
1.	Indian	55	63.22
2.	Imported	12	13.79
3.	Both	20	22.99
	Total	**87**	**100.00**

Source: Primary data.

It is observed that 63.22 per cent of the fishnet units have installed Indian made machineries and only a few fishnet units, that is 13.74 per cent units, have installed imported machineries. Another 20 units out of the total 87 fishnet units (22.99%) have both imported and domestically made machineries. Thus, it can be concluded from the above table that only a few of the fishnet units are capable of investing in foreign machines and adopting to latest technology. As a result, most of the fishnet unit's growth rate can be rated low in terms of adoption of latest technology.

ASSET BACKGROUND OF THE FAMILY

Successes of an enterprise depend upon the entrepreneurs and their asset background. Those entrepreneurs with sound asset background invest heavy amounts in the industry. Those entrepreneurs without any basic background cannot invest more in the business. Similarly, the loss and the risk which may arise in the business are easily borne by the entrepreneurs with sound asset background. The entrepreneurs with sound asset background face even the loss to the business on such occasions and the entrepreneur will not hesitate to invest from their pockets. These entrepreneurs who do not have sufficient asset background cannot go for investing more money. Hence, the family assets of the entrepreneurs act as a cushion to the entrepreneur. The eventualities happening in the business are borne by the family assets. Hence, asset backing of the family becomes a factor influencing growth in fishnet units. Table 5.20 deals with the detailed study on family asset background of the entrepreneurs of the fishnet units.

Table 5.20: Family Asset Background of the Fishnet Owners

Sl. No.	Asset Value	Number of Units	Percentage
1.	Below 100 Lakhs	59	67.82
2.	100 to 200 Lakhs	19	21.83
3.	200 to 300 Lakhs	5	5.75
4.	300 to 400 Lakhs	2	2.30
5.	400 to 500 Lakhs	2	2.30
	Total	**87**	**100.00**

Source: Primary data.

It is observed that, out of 87 fishnet units, 67.82 per cent (59 units) of the entrepreneurs have the family assets below Rs. 100 lakhs, 21.83 per cent (19 units) of the entrepreneurs have the family assets ranging from Rs. 100 to 200 lakhs, 5.75 per cent (5 units) have family assets ranging from Rs. 200 to 300 lakhs, 2.30 per cent (2 units) from Rs. 300 to 400 lakhs and the remaining 2.30 per cent(2 units) have family assets background of Rs. 400 to 500 lakhs. It shows that in Kanyakunmari district majority of the fishnet owners have the family assets up to Rs. 100 lakhs.

SOCIAL STATUS OF THE ENTREPRENEURS

The status what the entrepreneur commands the society has a role on the growth of their business units. The social status of an entrepreneur here means serving the society as panchayat president, union chairman, union member, M.L.A., M.P and the like. The position that an entrepreneur gain by becoming a member of Lions club, Rotary club, office bearer in community and religion based organisations also make them efficient administrators. Those entrepreneurs who command high respect in the society by virtue of their position in the society are able to achieve high growth in their undertaking. The experience and efficiency what they gain from their social status make them to run their units successfully. Hence, entrepreneurs having good social status achieve higher growth while the others show either a low growth or negative growth in their enterprises.

The social status of the entrepreneurs running fishnet units in Kanyakumari district are presented in Table 5.21.

Table 5.21: Social Status of the Entrepreneurs

Sl. No.	Status of Holding Position	Number of units	Percentage
1.	Not having position	58	66.67
2.	Having position	29	33.33
	Total	87	100.00

Source: Primary data.

Out of 87 fishnet units, 66.77 per cent (58 units) units entrepreneurs do not hold any positions in government/non government organisation and the remaining 33.33 per cent (29 units) hold some positions or have the experience of holding positions like M.P, M.L.A, Panchayat union president, panchayat union members, Rotarians, members of lions club and the like. It shows that in Kanyakumari district, majority of the entrepreneurs of fishnet units have not held any positions and thus they are lacking in leadership qualities.

FACTOR ANALYSIS—ANALYSIS AND INTERPRETATION

In order to identify the most influential factors contributing towards the growth of fishnet units in Kanyakumari district, the researcher has applied factor analysis. Rotated Component Matrix of factor Analysis helps to reduce the unmanageable numbers of variables into manageable number of variables called factors. It is a data reduction technique whereby the available variables are reduced to limited number of factors. All the above discussed 21 variables identified to be influencing the growth of fishnet units have been analysed through Factor analysis. The data was fed to the computer and the analysis was made through SPSS package. In the 21 variables have been reduced to five factors. But the level of influence that each variable has on these five factors is different from factor to factor. While a few variables have influenced much in a particular factor, the same do not influence so in some other factors. The influence that each variable has on each factor and the influence of all the five factors on the dependent variables indicating the growth of fishnet units have been analysed and the observation is presented in Table 5.22.

Table 5.22: Factors Promoting Growth of Fishnet Units—Factor Analysis—Rotated Component Matrix

Sl. No.	Variable	Component					Communality
		1	2	3	4	5	
1.	Period of credit allowed for raw material puchase	.775	-.232	.306	-6.903E-02	3.856E-02	0.275
2.	External liabilities of the entrepreneurs	-.738	-.222	-.152	7.226E-02	-.117	0.214
3.	Type of formation	.461	-.187	-.343	-3.340E-02	-.200	0.168
4.	Availability of raw material	-.405	-.209	-4.89E-03	-1.917E-02	.260	0.581
5.	Availability of skilled man power	.127	.714	-.231	-3.598E-02	1.286E-02	0.539
6.	Community Entrepreneurship	-.105	.578	-1.408E-02	4.996E-02	9.798E-02	0.406
7.	Educational qualification	-7.57E-02	-.490	-2.883E-02	-.101	-2.839E-02	0.454
8.	Type of family support	-4.596E-02	-.179	.652	.396	-6.671E-02	0.621
9.	Advertising in fishnet units	-2.593E-02	.140	.524	4.477E-03	.114	0.205
10.	Generation of ownership	.508	-.337	-.519	.225	5.943E-02	0.258
11.	Availability of infrastructural facilities	-.117	.108	-.418	1.161E-02	.118	0.695
12.	Uninterrupted power supply	8.031E-02	-8.973E-02	.383	-8.174E-02	2.176E-02	0.358
13.	Previous experience in the fishnet industries	-.229	-3.017E-02	-.101	.640	-.257	0.414
14.	Localisation advantage	.286	-5.408E-04	-9.314E-02	.547	.255	0.636
15.	Capacity utilisation	-4.403E-02	.302	.119	.535	-.116	0.718
16.	Social status of the entrepreneurs	5.932E-02	.290	.310	.533	.176	0.308
17.	Types of machinery	2.940E-02	.285	.244	-.384	-.124	0.561
18.	Expansion of marketing area of operation	-.109	-.316	-6.989E-02	6.037E-03	.736	0.659
19.	Export subsidy	-4.948E-02	-.276	3.983E-02	172	-.672	0.304
20.	Asset background of the family	-7.147E-02	.190	.289	.161	.501	0.401

(Contd…)

Sl. No.	Variable	Component					Communality
		1	2	3	4	5	
21.	Type of competition	.292	7.813E-02	-7.018E-02	7.740E-02	.321	0.499
	Eigen value	2.235	2.112	1.722	1.609	1.598	
	Variance	10.645	10.057	8.200	7.660	7.608	
	Cumulative	10.645	20.702	28.903	36.563	44.171	

Extraction method: Principal component and analysis, Rotation method: Varimax with Kaiser normalisation, a. rotation converged in 9 iterations.

Extraction method : Principal component Analysis

Rotation Method : Varimax with Kaiser Normalisation

a. Rotation converged in 9 iterations

The suitability of the data for factor analysis was analysed through Kaiser-Mayer-Olkin measure of adequacy and Bartlett's of sphericity tests. The findings of the test are:

Kaiser-Mayer-Olkin measure of sampling adequacy = 0.699			
Bartlett's of Sphericity:			
	Approx. Chi-square	:	301.503
	Df	:	210.000
	Sig	:	0.000

KMO test is a statistics which indicates the proportion of variance in the variables which might be caused by the underlying factors. The result of the test is a high value (0.699). This indicates that the factor analysis is useful for the data used in the study.

Bartlett's test of sphericity indicates whether the correlation matrix is an identity matrix. If it is so, an identity matrix and the variable identified are unrelated. The significance level gives the result of the test. Since the result is less than 0.05 it can be concluded that there is a significant relationship among the variables identified. Hence, it all shows that factor analysis can suitably employed in the study.

Table 5.22 shows the factor loading of the 21 variables influencing the growth in fishnet units. The factor analysis reduced the 21 variables into five factors namely F_1, F_2, F_3, F_4, and F_5.

The factors so categorised comprises of many variables. The variables fall under each category of factor in a way closely related to one another. The different factors so categorised are:

(i) Production factor

(ii) Employee factor

(iii) Background of the owner Factor

(iv) Marketing factor

(v) Competition factor

The production factor includes the variables namely raw materials purchased and period of credit availed. These two variables have a higher factor loading in the rotated component matrix. Production is the first factor which explains a higher variation of 10.645 per cent in the total variable set. The second factor employee represents the availability of skilled manpower and community of the fishnet owners. The employee factor also has a higher factor loading in the rotated component matrix. The employee factor explains higher variation of 10.057 per cent in the total variable set. The third factor, background of the owners, includes the variables namely family support, generation of ownership and previous experience of the owner. This factor also has a higher factor loading in the rotated component matrix. This explains a higher variation of 8.200 per cent in the total variable set. Marketing is the fourth factor which includes the variables namely social status, growth in capacity utilisation and expansion of marketing area. The marketing factor also has the next higher factor loading in rotated component matrix. The marketing factor explains a variation of 7.660 per cent in the total variable set. Finally, the competition factor accounts for a variation of .7.608 per cent in the total variable set. The competition factor includes the variables such as advanced machinery, type of competition and their localisation.

The eigen value of the factor indicates the degree of variability of the factor in the total set. The higher eign value shows the higher intensity of the variable explained in the factor.

Analysis of eigen values of different factors reveals the intensity of each factor comprising of 21 variables and their influence on the growth of fishnet units in Kanyakumari district. The eigen values of the factors such as production factor, employee factor, background of the owner factor, marketing factor and competition factor were 2.235, 2.112, 1.722, 1.609, and 1.598 respectively. It shows the intensity of the variables included in each factor. The intensity is higher in respect of production factor (2.235) and employee factor (2.112).

The communality *(h^2)* represents the role of each variable on the growth of fishnet units in Kanyakumari district. The communality has been high in respect of V_{13}, that is capacity utilisation, with communality value of 0.718, followed by *V2* infrastructural facilities for production with communality value of 0.695. It is followed by V_{18} expansion of marketing area of operation with communality value of 0.659, V_8 type of family support with the communality value of 0.621, V_1 availability of raw material with the communality value of 0.581, V_{19} usage of advanced machinery with the communality value of 0.561 and V_4 availability of skilled manpower with the communality value of 0.539. It exhibits that individually the variables such as capacity utilisation, infrastructural facilities for production, expansion of market area of operation, type of family support, availability of raw material, usage of advanced machinery and availability of skilled manpower are powerful in the order as presented here on the growth of fishnet units in Kanyakumari district.

In brief, factor analysis abridged the numerous unmanageable 21 variables into five manageable factors and shows their respective role on the growth of fishnet units in Kanyakumari district.

The linear multiple regression equation is fitted for each set of variables loaded in the factors which are responsible for growth. The mathematical forms of the regression equation framed for each factor are presented below:

(i) Production Factor

The two variables namely external liabilities of the entrepreneurs and period of credit allowed for raw material purchase are loaded in this factor. The regression equation framed for production factor is

$$y = 8.832 + 0.52x_1 + 0.537x_2$$

The regression co-efficient details relating to the production factor are presented in Table 5.23.

Table 5.23: Details of Regression Co-efficient Relating to Production Factor

Sl. No.	Variable name	Symbol	*b* value
1.	External liabilities of the entrepreneurs	x_1	0.52
2.	Period of credit allowed for raw material purchase	x_2	0.537
3.	Regression constant	b_0	8.832

Source: Primary data.

R square = 0.972

Sample size = 87

Analysis of multiple regression co-efficient relating to production factor reveals that the co-efficient of determination of regression between the variables external liabilities of the entrepreneurs and period of credit allowed for raw material purchase and the growth is 97 per cent It indicates that 97 per cent of the variation on the growth of fishnet units is influenced by the variables external liabilities of the entrepreneurs and period of credit allowed for raw material purchase. Analysis of the individual variables shows that for a unit change in external liabilities of the entrepreneurs, there is a change of 0.52 times on the growth of fishnet units. Similarly, for an unit of change in the variable period of credit allowed for raw material purchase, there is a change of 0.537 times on the growth of fishnet units. Hence, it can be concluded that both variables have a similar influence on the growth of fishnet units in Kanyakumari district.

(ii) Employee Factor

The two variables namely availability of skilled man power and community entrepreneurship are loaded in this factor. The regression equation framed for employee factor is

$$y = 6.612 + 0.6x_3 + 0.9x_4$$

The regression co-efficient details relating to the employee factor are presented in Table 5.24.

Table 5.24: Details of Regression Co-efficient Relating to Employee Factor

Sl. No.	Variable name	Symbol	*b* value
1.	Availability of skilled man power	x_3	0.6
2.	Community entrepreneurship	x_4	0.9
3.	Regression constant	b_0	0.612

Source: Primary data.

R square = 0.40

Sample size = 87

Analysis of multiple regression co-efficient relating employee factor reveals that the co-efficient of determination of regression between the variables availability of skilled man power and community entrepreneurship and the growth is 40 per cent. It indicates that 40 per cent of the variation on the growth of fishnet units is influenced by the variables availability of skilled man power and community entrepreneurship. Analysis of the individual variables shows that for an unit change in availability of skilled manpower there is a change of 0.60 times on the growth of fishnet units. Similarly, for on unit of change in the community entrepreneurship there is a change 0.9 times on the growth of fishnet units. Hence, it can be concluded that both variables have a similar influence on the growth of fishnet units in Kanyakumari district.

(iii) Background of the Entrepreneur Factor

The three variables namely type of family support, type of formation and generation of ownership are loaded in this factor. The regression co-efficient equation framed for background of the entrepreneur factor is

$$y = 4.785 + 0.65x_5 + 0.43x_6 + 0.72x_7$$

The regression co-efficient details relating to the background of the entrepreneur factor are presented in Table 5.25.

Analysis of multiple regression co-efficient relating background of the entrepreneur factors reveals that the co-efficient of determination of regression between the variables type of family support, types of formation and generation of ownership and the growth is 56 per cent. It indicates that 56 per cent of the variation on the growth of fishnet units is influenced by the variables type of family support, types of formation and generation of ownership. Analysis of the individual variables shows that for an unit change

Table 5.25: Details of Regression Co-efficient Relating to Background of the Entrepreneur Factor

Sl. No.	Variable name	Symbol	*b* value
1.	Type of family support	x_5	0.65
2.	Types of formation	x_6	0.43
3.	Generation of ownership	x_7	0.72
4.	Regression constant	b_n	4.785

Source: Primary data.

R square = 0.56
Sample size = 87

in type of family support there is a change of 0.65 times on the growth of fishnet units. Similarly, for an unit of change in the variable types of formation, there is a change of 0.43 times on the growth of fishnet units and for an unit of change in the variable generation of ownership, there is a change of 0.72 times on the growth of fishnet units. Hence, it can be concluded that al the three variables have a similar influence on the growth of fishnet units in Kanyakumari district.

(iv) Marketing Factor

There are four variables namely previous experience in the fishnet industry, localisation advantage, capacity utilisation and social status of the entrepreneurs are loaded in this factor. The regression co-efficient equation framed for marketing factor is

$$y = 5.943 + 0.42x_8 + 0.68x_9 + 0.51x_{10} + 0.621x_{11}$$

The regression co-efficient details relating to marketing factor are presented in Table 5.26.

Table 5.26: Details of Regression Co-efficient Relating to Marketing Factor

Sl. No.	Variable name	Symbol	*b* value
1.	Previous experience in the fishnet industry	x_8	0.42
2.	Localisation advantage	x_9	0.68
3.	Capacity utilisation	x_{10}	0.51
4.	Social status of the entrepreneur	x_{11}	0.621
5.	Regression constant	b_0	5.943

Source: Primary data.

R square = 0.62
Sample size = 87

Analysis of multiple regression co-efficient relating marketing factor reveals that the co-efficient of determination of regression between the variables previous experience in the fishnet industry, localisation advantage, capacity utilisation and social status of the entrepreneur and the growth is 62 per cent. It indicates that 62 per cent of the variation on the growth of fishnet units is influenced by the variables previous experience in the fishnet industry, localisation advantage, capacity utilisation and social status of the entrepreneur. Analysis of the individual variables shows that for an unit change in previous experience in the fishnet industry, there is a change of 0.42 times on the growth of fishnet units. Similarly, for on unit of change in the variable localisation advantage, there is a change of 0.68 times on the growth of fishnet units and for an unit of change in the variable capacity utilisation, there is a change of 0.51 times on the growth of fishnet units and an unit of change in the variable social status of the entrepreneur, there is a change of 0.621 times on the growth of fishnet units. Hence, it can be concluded that all the four variables have a similar influence on the growth of fishnet units in Kanyakumari district.

(v) Competition Factor

The three variables namely expansion of marketing area of operation, export subsidy and asset background of the family are loaded in this factor. The regression co-efficient equation framed for competition factor is

$$y = 10.982 + 0.34x_{12} + 0.743x_{13} + 0.449x_{14}$$

The regression co-efficient details relating to the competition factor are presented in Table 5.27.

Table 5.27: Details of Regression Co-efficient Relating to Competition Factor

Sl. No.	Variable name	Symbol	b value
1.	Expansion of marketing area of operation	x_{12}	0.34
2.	Export subsidy	x_{13}	0.743
3.	Asset background of the family	x_{14}	0.449
5.	Regression constant	b_0	10.982

Source: Primary data.

R square = 0.65

Sample size = 87

Analysis of multiple regression co-efficient relating competition factor reveals that the co-efficient of determination of regression between the variables expansion of marketing area of operation, export subsidy and asset background of the family and the growth is 65 per cent. It indicates that 65 per cent of the variation on the growth of fishnet units is influenced by the variables expansion of marketing area of operation, export subsidy and asset background of the family. Analysis of the individual variables shows that for an unit of change in expansion of marketing area of operation, there is a change of 0.34 times on the growth of fishnet units. Similarly, for an unit change in the variable export subsidy, there is a change of 0.743 time on the growth of fishnet units and for an unit of change in the variable asset background of the family, there is a change of 0.449 times on the growth of fishnet units. Hence, it can be concluded that all the three variables have a similar influence on the growth of fishnet units in Kanyakumari district.

SUMMARY

In this study, 21 variables have been identified to ascertain the growth of fishnet industrial units in Kanyakumari district. With the help of classification tables, the relationship between 21 variables and the growth of fishnet industrial units has been studied. The factor analysis employed in the study shows the inter-relationship among the variables and their influence on the growth of fishnet industrial units.

The 21 factors identified as the factors promoting growth of fishnet units have been short listed into five factors by applying the rotation matrix and confirm matrix. They are production factor, employee factor, background of the owners, marketing factor and competition factor. The production factor is the first factor which explains a higher variation in the total variable set which is followed by the employee factor. The eigen values representing the interesting of the variables included in the factors are also higher in these cases. These two factors are followed by background of the owners factor, marketing factor and competition factor in terms of the factor loadings in rotated component matrix.

The communality (h^2) representing the role of each variable on the growth of fishnet units exhibits that individually, the variables such as capacity utilisation, infrastructural facilities for production, expansion of market area of operation, type of family support, availability of raw material, usage of advanced machinery and availability of skilled manpower are powerful on the growth of fishnet units in Kanyakumari district.

REFERENCES

1. Sri Vastava, T.N., Shailaja Rego, *Statistics for Management Analysis*, TATA McGraw-Hill Publishing Company Limited, New Delhi, 2008, pp. 9.11-9.12.
2. Kothari, C.R., *Research Methodology—Methods and Techniques*, New Age International Pvt., Publisher, 2006, p. 323.

3. Harry H. Harman, *Modern Factor Analysis*, The University of Chicago Press, 1967, pp. 97-101.

4. Thurstone, L. and Chava, E., *The Measurement of Attitude*, The University of Chicago Press, 1929, pp. 508-509.

5. *Ibid.*, p. 93.

6. Benjamine, Fruether, *Introduction of Factor Analysis*, New Delhi, Affiliated East-West Press, 1976, p. 106.

7. Fred N. Kertenger, *Methods of Factor Analysis*, Foundation of Behavioural Research, NewYork, Holt Rinchart and Winston Inc., 1973, p. 470.

8. Khanka, S.S., *Entrepreneurial Development*, S. Chand Company Ltd., New Delhi, 2008, pp. 240-241.

9. Khanka, S.S., *op.cit.*, pp. 240-241.

Summary of Findings Problems and Suggestions

INTRODUCTION

The present study is an attempt to find out the growth of fishnet units in Kanyakumari district. The main thrust of the study is measuring the growth achieved by fishnet units and locating the factors promoting industrial growth in fishnet units. While studying the growth, the factors which promote growth have also been analysed. The findings made in the study have been quiet interesting. In this chapter, the researcher presents the summary of the findings of the study. At the end part of the chapter, suggestions for achieving a higher growth in fishnet units in Kanyakumari district have been given.

The approach to the study has been both descriptive and analytical. The researcher conveniently used both the primary and secondary data for the preparation of the thesis. For collecting the primary data, the researcher has used a structured questionnaire. Census method has been used to collect the information from 114 respondents who run fishnet units in Kanyakumari district. The list of 114 entrepreneurs supplied by the District Industrial Centre, Nagercoil. The researcher made an attempt to cover all the 114 entrepreneurs but only 87 entrepreneurs responded to the study. Hence, the study is confined to 87 entrepreneurs running fishnet units in Kanyakumari district. Officials belonging to the Department of Fisheries, Government of Tamil Nadu, Industrial owners who have had long years of experience in managing fishnet units, and office bearers of the Fishnet Manufacturers Association and a selected group of academicians who had association with fishnet units have been consulted. The suggestions presented in this study are based on the discussions the researcher has had with the above mentioned experts on different occasions.

SUMMARY OF FINDINGS

The study measures the growth of fishnet units through the data collected from the entrepreneurs of fishnet units in Kanyakumari district through a structured questionnaire. Besides the data collected through the questioners, the informal discussions with the employees of the fishnet units were also helpful in identifying the variables for measuring the growth of fishnet units. The findings of the study are summarised below.

FISHNET INDUSTRY

While reviewing the history of fishnet industry it is found that fishing has a long history in the Indian Coastline. Fishnet has been an important implement used in fish catching. The traditional fishnets were made up of cotton yarn. Due to technological advancements, now synthetic nylon filaments are used in the manufacture of fishnet. Modernisation of fishnets has increased the productivity in fishing. Further, modernisation of fishnet has made the fishing sector efficient. The introduction of modern technologies in fishing crafts and gears has created social unrest among the fisher-folk.

Synthetic fibre (nylon filament) was first used for fishing in Japan in 1932. The cotton and hemp used for the last 30 years were then replaced by nylon yarn. As a result of improvement in the quality of the raw materials and advancement in net making techniques, mass production was attained resulting in reduction in cost.

Fishnet industry comprises of two major sub-sectors namely making of nylon yarns and manufacturing fishnet. Over a period of time. Indian fishery sector has made rapid growth in terms of production, income and exports. There are different types of nets used for catching fish in different countries. Specific categories of fishnets are used exclusively for catching specific categories of fishes. Different types of nets used for fishing have different qualities. The popular Types of fishnets in use are handnet, cast net, chinese net, gillnet, drift net, stake net, trammel, trawl net, fixed or stationary nets, dip nets and bag nets. Among these gears, all types are not used in Tamil Nadu. The popular types of gears used in Tamil Nadu for fishing are trawl net, gillnet, scene net, bag net, drift nets and hooks and line.

On the basis of the raw materials used in fishnet making, fishnets are classified as monofilament fishnets and multifilament fishnets. Fishnets made out of monofilament (single filament) are referred as monofilament fishnet, while in multifilament fishnet, more than one filament is used. Monofilament fishnet using monofilament yarn as raw material is not durable like the other type. The standard sizes of thickness of monofilament fishnets ranges from 0.12 mm to 0.23 mm. The processes involved in making nylon monofilament yarn are blending, melting, spinning, cooling, stretching, annealing, oiling, winding and packing. In multifilament fishnet, two or three filaments are twisted together to form a multifilament twine which is used in making multifilament fishnet. Higher the number of filaments twisted the greater is the strength the net has. The standard sizes of multifilament fishnet are 1/2 are 1/3. In the multifilament fishnet of the type 1/2, two filaments of varying sizes are twisted together to form a single twine which is used in fishnet making. But in the 1/3 multifilament fishnet, three filaments are twisted together to form a single twine, used in fishnet making.

Fishnets are also classified on the basis of the knots used in the fishnets. Knots are the knitting arrangement of yarns in fishnet making. The popular models of knots used in fishnet making are single knot and double knot. Double knot is stronger than single knot. There are different types of machinery used for making different types of fishnet.

The history of fishnet units in Kanyakumari district shows that fishnet units have a very recent origin in the district after 1990's. Fishnet industry is a small scale industry which provides employment to nearly 40,000 people in Kanyakumari district. Mr. Haizar Abdul Majeed is the pioneer in fishnet industry in the district. The first nylon fishnet unit was established in Kanyakumari district at Manavalakurichi in 1975. Though the first fishnet unit has established in 1975 the industry has not progressed well till 1990. During the period from 1990 to 2000 there was a phenomenal growth of fishnet industry in Kanyakumari district.

GROWTH OF FISHNET INDUSTRY

Growth means improvement, enhancement, development, and forward progress. In business, growth means growing in size in terms of net worth and asset backing resulting in addition of product line. The growth is attained at two levels:

(i) Horizontal growth; and

(ii) Vertical growth.

There are ten variables identified as the indicators of the growth of fishnet industry in Kanyakumari district. They are: gross profit, net profit, production capacity, sales, capacity utilised, capital employed, number of employees, assets owned, external liabilities and raw material utilised. The growth of fishnet units in Kanyakumari district was measured through Compound Growth Rate (CGR). The analysis reveals that majority of units (52.87%) in Kanyakumari district have not attained any growth in terms of gross profit. Among the 87 fishnet units surveyed, only (45.98%) of the units have showed growth. The reason is, even though in the initial years the fishnet units had earned huge gross profit, in recent years they could not maintain it so because of competition.

It is further observed in the study that majority of the fishnet units (63.22%) in Kanyakumari district have not achieved growth in terms of net profit. Only five per cent of the fishnet units have shown positive growth. The reasons attributable for this dismal performance of fishnet units in terms of net profit are the increasing administrative and financial cost.

The production capacity is another variable in relation to which the growth of fishnet units is assessed. It is clear from analysis that 57.47 per cent of fishnet units have shown positive growth in terms of capacity. The growth ranges between zero to five per cent. The negative growth was high among rest of the fishnet units in Kanyakumari district. It is found that 42.53 per cent of the units have recorded a negative growth, which ranges between zero and -5 per cent. Evaluation of growth of fishnet units in terms of production capacity reveals that only a section of the total fishnet units in Kanyakumari district have grown. But the growth was not significant. The same view is supplemented by the negative growth recorded by the other section of fishnet units. It all shows that though fishnet units have grown marginally in terms of production capacity, the growth is not significant.

Another variable measuring the growth of fishnet units is volume of sales. Sales volume has grown well in fishnet units in Kanyakumari district. It is interesting to find that most of the units have shown a positive growth in terms of sales. It is observed that 92 per cent of the fishnet units have shown a positive growth in terms of sales which ranges from zero to 10 per cent. The main reason for the increase in sales volume in the past 10 years is that the demand for fishnet is growing steadily due to mechanisation of the fishing crafts and expansion of local market to the state level.

Capacity utilisation by the fishnet units in Kanyakumari district shown by fishnet units in Kanyakumari district shows that 85 units (97.70%) have shown a positive growth in terms of capacity utilisation which ranges between zero to above 10 per cent. Only two units showed a negative growth. The reasons for the growth of capacity utilisation are increase in sales volume, uninterrupted supply of raw materials and expansion of market.

It is identified in the study that most of the fishnet units in Kanyakumari district have shown a negative growth in terms of capital employed. Sixty two units (71.26%) functioning in Kanyakumari district have recorded a negative growth ranging from -10 to zero per cent in terms of capital employed in the last 10 years. Only 28.74 per cent of the units have witnessed positive growth ranging between zero per cent to 25 per cent. Capital employed has not become a significant variable in the last 10 years in Kanyakumari district. The reason for the negative growth of capital employed in fishnet units in Kanyakumari district implies the non introduction of additional capital and non ploughback of profits by the entrepreneurs of the fishnet units in Kanyakumari district.

Analysis of the growth of number of persons employed in the fishnet units reveals that more than half of the units studied (58.58%) have achieved only a negative growth. Around 49.42 per cent of the units have shown a positive growth in terms of employment generation. Only one unit has registered a growth of 20 per cent to 25 per cent. The main reason for negative growth of employees in fishnet units in Kanyakumari district is the high turnover of employees. For various reasons turnover has been high in the sector in Kanyakumari district. Non-availability of transport facilities, absence of good remuneration package and other facilities could have been the main reasons prompting the employees to resign their job.

It is identified that around 57.42 per cent of fishnet units in Kanyakumari district have registered a growth ranging up to 15 per cent in terms of assets. Thirty seven units (42.53%) had a negative growth rate in terms of asset. The main reason for the negative growth rate is the closure of existing units due to repairs and obsolescence of machines used. Obsolescence of machinery and major repairs depreciated the value of assets year by years. Thus, the value of assets showed a negative growth over years.

It is further located that in most of the units (73.56%), the growth in terms of external liabilities is negative. It is ranging from zero to (-) 20 per cent. Twenty three units (26.44%) in Kanyakumari district have achieved a positive growth which is ranging up to 20 per cent. The reason for this trend is the lack of supply of finance from external sources like bank and government agencies.

It is identified that raw material utilisation shows a positive growth in relation to 70 units. The rate of growth ranged up to 25 per cent. Another 19.54 per cent of the units have a negative growth ranging up to (-) 20 per cent. The reason for the growth of fishnet units in terms of raw material utilisation in Kanyakumari district is the uninterrupted supply of raw materials. Since majority of the fishnet units engaged in fishnet manufacturing have their own units to supply yarns, production is uninterrupted throughout the year individual growth so calculated for each fishnet unit through various variables are comprehended through a growth scale.

ENTREPRENEURSHIP AND GROWTH

Entrepreneurship plays a significant role in industrial development. Entrepreneur perceives a need and then brings together the manpower, materials and capital required to meet the need. An entrepreneur is the backbone of an industry and its growth depends upon its entrepreneurs. Entrepreneurial growth and industrial growth are closely related. Entrepreneur refers to a person who establishes his/her own business or industrial undertaking with a view to making profit. Thus, entrepreneur is always action oriented, he/she is both a thinker and doer; planner and worker, accepts risk and manages it. A good and efficient entrepreneur successfully run an industrial enterprise and achieves growth. Growth of an industrial unit mainly depends upon its entrepreneur. Hence, entrepreneurial variables have a relationship with the growth of the industrial unit. Taking this fact into account, the relationship between entrepreneurship and growth of the industrial unit is separately analysed. The researcher has identified ten variables as related to entrepreneurship as having relationship with the growth of fishnet units. The variables are community, religion, reasons for starting the units, nature of ownership, forms of organisation, period of establishment, number of machineries installed, varieties of product manufactured, capital contributed by the owner (owned capital) and number of shifts worked. These variables have a significant role in the determination of entrepreneurial performance *vis-á-vis* industrial growth. The fishnet units managed by the entrepreneurs with immense entrepreneurial talents are able to achieve better than the others and the others could not so achieve because of their deficiencies.

Analysis of the communal setting of the entrepreneur reveals that most of the entrepreneurs of fishnet units (75.86%) in Kanyakumari district belong to non-fishermen communities. It is interesting to note that the fishnet units run by entrepreneurs having from non-fishermen communities have achieved a better growth than the entrepreneurs from fishermen community. Statistical testing through Chi-square test also approved that the community of the entrepreneurs has become an important variable which has a significant relationship with the growth of fishnet units.

Another variable which is identified for the analysis of growth is religion. It is found in the study that a majority of the fishnet entrepreneurs in Kanyakumari district (56 units) belongs to Christianity. It is observed that the growth units and non-growth units are equal in number (28 units) in case of Christian entrepreneurs and the growth is very low among the Hindu entrepreneurs. In case of muslim entrepreneurs, nearly one-third of the units have recorded growth. Statistical testing through Chi-square test shows that the religion of the entrepreneurs is not a variable having relationship with growth.

The growth of the fishnet unit has a relationship with the reason for starting the industrial unit. It is identified that in fishnet industry in Kanyakumari district less than one-third of the entrepreneurs have started their units out of compulsions and majority of the entrepreneurs (41.38 per cent) have started their units with real entrepreneurial spirits such as to be self-employed and capitalising their previous experience. It is observed that the growth is high among the units started with previous experience in the business and it is very low among the units started out of family compulsions. The Chi-square test identified that various reasons for starting the fishnet units do not have a relationship with their growth.

Analysis of the nature of ownership shows that in Kanyakumari district three-fourth of the fishnet units is owned establishments of the entrepreneurs. The growth is high in case of hired fishnet units and it is very low among the leased units. The growth is observed to be low in case of first category of fishnet units. But statistical testing through Chi-square test identified that the type of ownership is not a major variable having influence in the growth of fishnet units in Kanyakumari district.

While analysing the forms of organisation of the fishnet units in Kanyakumari district, it is observed that a majority of the fishnet units (72.41%) in Kanyakumari district are in the form of sole proprietorship. Analysis of growth reveals that growth is higher in case of sole proprietorship, entrepreneurs compared to units with other forms of organization such as partnership and private limited company. But statistical analysis through Chi-square test reveals that the forms of ownership are not a major variable having influence on the growth of fishnet units.

In the study, it is found that those units established before 2000 AD earned a good profit and show a higher growth and those which were started after 2000 AD are not able to show better growth. Analysis of growth achieved by fishnet units in Kanyakumari district reveals that growth is high among the units established earlier before 2000 AD compared to those established recently. The same is approved by Chi-square test.

In the study it is found that, in most of the fishnet units in Kanyakumari district, the number of machineries used is ranging between one to three. The growth is found comparatively higher among the fishnet units with more number of machineries. But testing of hypothesis did not approve it. It is found that the number of machineries used is not a major variable related to growth in fishnet units.

Most of the fishnet units (43.68%) in Kanyakumari district are producing mono filament single knot fishnets. Yarns used in manufacturing of fishnets are produced by a few units only. It is observed that the growth is high among the units producing monofilament fishnet. Compared to the other units producing other types of products, the growth it is very low among the units producing yarn. But statistical test viz; Chi-square test did not approve it and it is found that the variety of products manufactured by the entrepreneurs is not a major variable which has relationship with growth.

With regard to capital contributed by the owner, it is found that in Kanyakumari district, most of the fishnet units (76 units) have the owned capital which ranges between Rs. 10 lakhs and Rs. 40 lakhs. It is observed that higher growth is registered by fishernet units with lower amount of owned capital compared to the units with higher amount of owned capital. The same relationship analysed through Chi-square test found that the relationship between the sizes of owned capital invested and the growth achieved by them do not have a significant relationship.

Analysis of growth reveals that growth is comparatively higher in case of the units with more shifts than the units functioning with less number of shifts. The main reason is that units working in the night shift (third shift) could not employ female workers. Because Factories Act does not permit women to work in night shift. The male workers works in the night shift do not show excellence in their work. Hence the production and productivity in the night shift is very low. This hampered the overall growth of fishnet units. But statistical testing through Chi-square test did not accept it. Instead, it is identified that the number of shifts worked does not have any relationship with the growth of fishnet units.

FACTORS PROMOTING GROWTH OF FISHNET INDUSTRY

Industrial growth is a common phenomenon in the newly started units and the existing ones. There are many factors which are promoting growth of fishnet units. It has been identified that there are 21 variables responsible for the growth of fishnet units in Kanyakumari district. Factor analysis has been employed to find out the level of influence of these factors on growth.

The variables identified as influencing growth in fishnet units are:

(a) Availability of raw material

(b) Availability of infrastructural facilities

(c) Uninterrupted power supply

(d) Availability of skilled manpower

(e) Previous experience in the fishnet industry

(f) Type of formation

(g) Localisation advantage

(h) Type of family support

(i) Type of competition

(j) Educational qualification

(k) Generation of ownership

(l) Community of the entrepreneurs

(m) Capacity utilisation

(n) External liabilities of the entrepreneur

(o) Period of credit allowed for raw material purchase

(p) Advertising in fishnet units

(q) Export subsidy availed

(r) Expansion of market area of operation

(s) Usage of advanced machinery

(t) Asset background of the family

(u) Social status of the entrepreneurs

Analysis of the variables promoting growth reveals that majority of the fishnet units (89.66 per cent) in Kanyakumari district enjoys the uninterrupted supply of raw materials. Hence, production is smooth without any interruption throughout the year whereas 10.34 per cent fishnet units are affected by non-availability of raw materials in the local area.

With regard to availability of infrastructural facilities, 87.36 per cent of the fishnet units functioning in Kanyakumari district have sufficient infrastructural facilities needed for production. Only 11 units out of 87 units have no sufficient infrastructural facilities.

It is further observed that most of the fishnet units in the study area (83.91%) (73 units) have the problem with regard to power supply. Another 16.19 per cent of the total fishnet units are not disturbed by shortage of power. The main reason for this trend is that fishnet units in Kanyakumari district have their own arrangement of generators to offset the problem.

Skilled labour is another variable with respect to which fishnet units suffer much. Hence, availability of skilled manpower has become a factor influencing growth in fishnet units in Kanyakumari district. It reveals that most of the fishnet units (54 units) in Kanyakumari district are troubled with non-availability of skilled manpower. Another 33 fishnet units studied in the study area are not affected by short supply of skilled manpower. The reason for short supply of skilled manpower, in Kanyakumari district is the frequent switchover of workers from one unit to other units which obstructs the units where from skilled workers switch over.

Another variable influencing growth in fishnet units is the experience of the owners of fishnet units. It is observed in the study that 45.97 per cent of fishnet unit owners have started their units without any experience in fishnet industry. Another 21 fishnet unit owners representing 24.14 per cent of the total units studied have business experience in other industries whereas, 29.89 per cent have the business experience in the same industry as a partner, supervisor, electrician and worker.

Inheritance of an existing unit by a successive entrepreneur makes the successor to show growth. Hence successive inheritance of business has become another factor influencing growth in fishnet units. Many of the fishnet units in the study area (72.41%) have been started by the entrepreneurs as new ventures. Another 10.34 per cent of the units have inherited the business from their forefathers and are run as family business units.

Localisation of fishnet units in a single cluster is another variable influencing growth in fishnet units. It is observed that most of the fishnet units in Kanyakumari district have been functioning either around A.N. Kudy or around Konam. Only 25 fishnet units have scattered over other places, such as Vellamody, Pudur, Manavalakurichi, Manikattipottal and other areas.

The support of the family to run the business is another factor influencing growth in fishnet units. It is significant to note that nearly two-third (70.11%) of the entrepreneurs of the fishnet units in Kanyakumari district have got the support of the family members. The other 29.89 per cent entrepreneurs did not receive any support from their family members.

In modern days, competition is an important factor promoting growth. It is identified that only 3 fishnet units (3.45%) in Kanyakumari district are not affected by competition. Analysis shows that 55.17 per cent (48 units) fishnet units experience price competition and a few other units face competition in terms of quality.

Literacy level of the entrepreneurs also provides growth in fishnet units run by them. It is very significant to note that no entrepreneurs in fishnet units Kanyakumari district are illiterate. More than half of the entrepreneurs (47 units) surveyed are graduates or post graduates or professionals. In the same way, entrepreneurs of 29 units (33.34%) have either passed +2 or SSLC. It reveals that the overall educational level of the entrepreneurs in fishnet industry in Kanyakumari district is good.

The generation of entrepreneurship is another factor influencing growth of fishnet units in Kanyakumari district. Out of 87 fishnet units, 89.66 per cent of the units are run by first generation entrepreneurs while 9 units (10.34%) are run by second generation entrepreneurs. Since Kanyakumari district is an industrially backward area, entrepreneurship is very slowly picking up. Most of the fishnet units in Kanyakumari district are run by first generation entrepreneurs.

Community to which the entrepreneurs belong is also a factor promoting growth of fishnet units. It reveals that a majority of entrepreneurs in the fishnet manufacturing units belong to non-fishermen communities. In the study, 75.86 per cent of the entrepreneurs of fishnet units in Kanyakumari district fall under this category. Only 21 units (24.14%) are run by entrepreneurs belong to the fishermen communities.

Capacity utilisation is another important factor promoting the growth of fishnet units. It is observed that among the fishnet units functioning in Kanyakumari district, 45 units representing (51.72%) have recorded a positive compound growth ranging between 5 and 10 per cent in terms of capacity utilisation in the last 10 years. Only 2.30 per cent fishnet units show a growth of 10 to 15 per cent. The main reasons for the slow growth of the fishnet units may be the growing competition and rising cost of raw materials.

The size of external liabilities indicates the size of investment made in the business. Therefore, it is also an indicator of growth of a business unit. It is identified that majority of (59.77%) the fishnet units are having external liabilities ranging between Rs. 25 lakhs and Rs. 50 lakhs. A very few 5.57 per cent fishnet units in Kanyakumari district are having external liabilities ranging between Rs. 75 lakhs to Rs. One crore. The reason for the increase in external liabilities is the increase in production capacity and number of machinery used.

A majority of the fishnet units (35.63%) in the study area have availed 15 days credit for raw material purchased from the suppliers. A few fishnet units (5 units) have availed 60 days period of credit. It shows that in Kanyakumari district majority of the fishnet units have availed a credit period which ranges up to 30 days.

The promotional measures like advertisement is an indication of a business enterprise's market expansion efforts. Therefore, it can be taken as an indicator of growth also. It is observed that only 8.05 per cent (7 units) of the fishnet units are involved in advertising. But a majority of (91.95%) the fishnet units advertises their product or company. It clearly records that only a countable number of fishnet units only the advertisement and rest of the units do not show any interest in advertising.

Export subsidy is given by the government to the units exporting their products. To export the product, the fishnet units have to maintain international standard in quality of the fishnets. Therefore, exports and the subsidy availed on it shall be taken as a growth indicators of fishnet units. The study reveals that 91.95 per cent of fishnet units in Kanyakumari district have not availed export subsidy. Only 7 units out of 87 units have availed export subsidy. The main reason for not availing the export subsidy is the lack of export orientation and lack of international quality of the product.

Market expansion is vital for business growth. Therefore, the market coverage of a business unit shall be considered as an indicator of its growth. If the market coverage increases, the business grows. In Kanyakumari district, a majority of the fishnet units have a market coverage at state level (44.83%) and national level (37.93%) and only a few industrial units (8 units) concentrate in the local market.

The investment made in machinery is another factor contributing towards the growth of an industrial unit. Because, investment in machinery determines the production capacity of the unit. The fishnet units use both foreign made and Indian made machines. Foreign made machines are costlier and qualitative. Their cost is five times higher than that of Indian made. Therefore, investments in foreign made machine shall be taken as an indicator of growth in fishnet units. The study discloses that 63.22 per cent of fishnet units in Kanyakumari district have installed Indian made machineries and only a few industries (12 units) have installed imported foreign machineries. Another 22.99 per cent entrepreneurs have installed both Indian made and imported machineries. The reason behind the large number of installation of Indian made machines was the higher cost of imported machines which ranges between. Rs. 40 to Rs. 70 lakhs where as it is very low in case of Indian machineries which ranges between Rs. 8 to Rs. 14 lakhs.

The family asset background of the entrepreneurs shows their financial solvency. Their personal assets and family assets add financial strength to their business, especially in case of sole-proprietorship form of business enterprises. Almost all entrepreneurs of fishnet units in Kanyakumari district have contributed their own capital to the business. Therefore, it is relevant to assess the growth the business unit by the family asset position of the entrepreneurs. The study reveals that 67.82 per cent (59 units) entrepreneurs have the family assets below Rs. 100 lakhs. A very few entrepreneurs, that is 2 units (2.30%) each, are having the family asset background of Rs. 300 to 400 lakhs and Rs. 400 to Rs. 500 lakhs respectively.

Social status of the entrepreneurs and their positions in government and non-governmental organisations influences their entrepreneurial abilities. Thus they also contribute towards the growth of the business enterprise. It is identified that 66.77 per cent (58 units) entrepreneurs of the fishnet units in Kanyakumari district do not hold any position in the society and only 29 entrepreneurs (33.33%) have held some positions in the society. Thus, it can be understood that the social status and the position of the entrepreneurs have not much influence on the growth of the fishnet units.

In order to reduce the above discussed number of variables into manageable number of factors and to study the level of influence of these variables over the growth, Factor Analysis was attempted. As the outcome, the following findings have come out. Factor analysis reduced the 21 variables into five factors namely *F1*, *F2*, *F3*, *F4* and *F5*. Different factors so categorized are:

(i) Production factor;

(ii) Employee factor;

(iii) Asset background;

(iv) Marketing factor; and

(v) Competition factor.

Production factor explains a higher variation of 10.645 per cent. The second factor Employee factor represents the next highest variation of 10.057 per cent. The third factor, background of the owner had a variation of 8.200 per cent. Marketing is the fourth factor which represents a variation of 7.660 per cent. Finally, the competition factor accounts for a variation of 7.608 per cent in the total variable set. The Eigen values of the factor indicate the degree of variability of the factor in the total set. The higher eigen value shows the higher intensity of the variables explained in the factor. The variables such as capacity utilisation, infrastructural facilities for production, expansion of market area operation, type of family support, availability of raw-material, usage of advanced machinery and availability of skilled manpower are powerful in the order and promoting growth of fishnet units in Kanyakumari district.

PROBLEMS AND SUGGESTIONS

The analytical exercise involved in the study is based entirely on documentary evidences and the primary data collected by the investigator from a carefully chosen set of informants. The study has thrown light on some specific problems. The various problems identified in the study and the suggestions to solve them are presented in this part. For each of the problem, the researcher has tried to find solutions to overcome.

This study based on the primary data collected by the investigator from the entrepreneurs of fishnet industrial units reveals the fact that majority of the fishnet units in Kanyakumari district have not achieved growth in terms of their financial investment status, production size, profitability and employability. Because, they encounter many problems which inhibit their growth. The problems which inhibit growth of fishnet units are explained below.

HIGHER COST OF ELECTRICITY AND INTERRUPTION IN POWER SUPPLY

Cost of power is one of the major elements of cost of production of fishnet. The cost per unit of electricity charged by TNEB has been steadily increasing over years. The 20 per cent power subsidy granted by the Tamil Nadu Electricity Board has also been stopped. Thus, the cost of power has increased manifold which ultimately results into higher cost of production. Further, the power cut in the district has also increased recently in terms of frequency and duration than in earlier days. This results into the need for having generators, which lead to additional fixed and running expenditure.

Moreover, the cost of fuel that is diesel, for running these generators is also increasing. All these results into the increase in production cost in general and the cost of power in specific. Thus, power problem faced by fishnet unit has impacted profitability of the fishnet units. Therefore, the researcher suggests that a guaranteed uninterrupted power supply should be assured by the government at a subsidised unit price. Further, the dropped subsidy scheme may be revived, whereby the cost of power will be reduced for fishnet units. In addition to these assistances, diesel used for power generation purpose may be provided at subsidised price, as is given to fisherfolk, to run generators in case of power cuts. The quota system based on the scale of operation of the fishnet units (number of machines run) may be introduced to fairly distribute diesel to all fishnet units.

DEFICIENCY OF SKILLED MANPOWER AND LABOUR TURNOVER

Lack of skilled and trained manpower is the most common problem face by most of the fishnet units in Kanyakumari district. Moreover, the turnover rate is high in fishnet industry. The turnover is a serious problem especially in job categories like electrical and mechanical work. There is no formal training offered to the technicians involved in fishnet making. Operators engaged in knitting machines and heating machines require formal training to operate their machines. Since trained technicians are not available, new ones are placed to operate the machines. Production is affected by such workers. The quality of the products manufactured is poor. Further, the production cost increases. The newly appointed untrained workers get training by their own or with the help of their co-workers. This leads to high amount of wastages. Sometimes, such new entrants face accidents.

To solve this problem it is suggested that formal training should be imparted to the unemployed youth through Government and private Industrial Training Institutes (ITI). Fishnet Producers Association may also offer such training to the new workers. The trainees may be given stipend for the training period so that more number of youth will be motivated to undergo the training. Sufficient publicity about the training programme may be given. In order to reduce the prevailing labour turnover in fishnet industry, the salary structure may be made attractive. The workers may be given a reasonable salary and other benefits such as provident fund and bonus. The association may fix common salary structure for the various categories of workers in fishnet units so that the turnover in the sector can be considerably reduced.

LOW MARGIN

The next important problem faced by the fishnet units is that very often the fishnet units are unable to get reasonable margin for their products. The wholesale buyer of fishnets is highly price conscious. Wholesale buyers have the power to fix the price for fishnet. Because, there is a tough competition prevailing among the manufacturers to supply fishnets at a cheaper price. Further, the foreign manufacturers are also competing in the market. As the competition in fishnet industry is increasing, buyers take the upper hand in fixing the prices. The small scale entrepreneurs, inorder to survive in the market, often compelled to sell their products at a price lesser than the cost. The competition among fishnet manufacturers reduces the profitability of the business. Moreover, the raw material prices are highly fluctuating and generally are on increasing trend. Thus, the cost of production is already very high. This adds fuel to the above problem. There is no price regulatory system to control the prices of raw material. The large scale entrepreneurs are able to gain the economies of large scale purchase and manage the problem to some extent. But, small scale units are highly affected by the growing prices of raw materials.

The researcher finds that strengthening the collective bargaining in raw material purchase is the solution to solve the problem related to prices of raw material. As a mechanism, the producers' association may form a cartel to purchase raw material needed for its members. Collective orders may be placed through the association whereby the purchase cost can be reduced.

In order to avoid the competition among producers in selling fishnets in the market, an arrangement as similar to purchase of raw material may be arranged for selling the fishnet. A pool may be organised by the fishnet manufacturers association. The pool may be formed as a separate agency engaged in marketing of fishnets manufactured by its members. In the pool, all fishnet units shall be the members. The pool so organised may employ marketing experts as its employees and professionalise their services. Further, the pool may either directly or through agents distributes fishnets not only in the state but also throughout the country. The pool may export the fishnets abroad. Professionalisation of marketing services increases sales and avoids unnecessary competition. It further safeguards the interest of the small scale fishnet units.

LACK OF QUALITY CONTROL SYSTEM

There is no quality control system in fishnet industry in Kanyakumari district. The quality of the fishnets is not standardised. Sometimes, substandard fishnets are even marketed in the market in the name of low prices. As the buyers are price conscious, the manufacturers sell inferior quality fishnets at lower prices. The quality is compromised for price by many of the manufacturers in the district. There is no quality standardisation mechanism or institution. Thus, the products of the fishnet units are not able to be marketed in international market. Hence, most of the fishnet units are price conscious. Manufacturing of substandard quality fishnets limits the growth of fishnet units. Substandard fishnets can not be marketed either in the national or global market. Hence, most of the fishnet units functioning in Kanyakumari district have been marketing their fishnets in the district alone. Rarely a few units are export oriented and the others are concentrating only about the local market. Products of such fishnet units are rejected on quality grounds from export. The fishnet units in the district do not have a long vision to go elsewhere and promote their business. Hence in a broader perspective fishnet units in Kanyakumari district are not functioning with long term perspective.

As quality is the main factor determining the marketability especially at international level, the researcher suggests that a good quality control mechanism should be introduced. Further, the quality of the fishnets is to be standardised. Government may come forward to establish a standardisation institute like ISI, ISO to supervise and control the quality standards of the fishnets. Otherwise, the existing institutions such as ISI and ISO may publish quality standards for fishnets. Further, the existing legal system may be amended so that all units shall have standard certification. Similarly, the Government may take initiative to popularise the need for standardisation among fishnet units so that the entrepreneurs shall be motivated in improving the quality of their products.

LACK OF EXPORT ORIENTATION

Most of the fishnets produced by the fishnet units in Kanyakumari district are sold within the country, mainly in North Indian markets such as the states of Maharastra and West Bengal and in many other Southern states such as Andhra Pradesh and Pondicherry. Only a few units are export oriented and two among the 87 units covered in the study are hundred per cent export oriented. Their exports too confined to Gulf and Asian countries. The potential demand in the global market is left untapped. There is a very minimum motivation among the entrepreneurs towards export. Most of them are lacking of knowledge and skills for export. Moreover, as the competition in the global market is quality oriented, the marketability of Indian fishnets is poor in the international market.

As a solution to solve this problem, it is suggested that Marine Products Exports Development Authority or any other similar agency of the Government of India may motivate the fishnet units to go for exporting the fishnets in the global market. As the first step, it may suggest means to improve the quality of the products to international standards. Entrepreneurs may be given proper orientation and training on global marketing. The Export Promotion Council of the Government of India may offer guidance to them to export. Further, the Government may offer special subsidies and concessions for exports and tax exemption on such export oriented production units.

NON-AVAILABILITY OF RAW MATERIALS LOCALLY

The raw material for fishnet units is nylon yarn. Nylon yarn is produced locally only by five units and their production is not sufficient to the requirement of the fishnet units in Kanyakumari district. For the rest of the requirements, the fishnet units have to depend on the suppliers from Coimbatore, Pondicherry and Delhi. The prices of yarn in these cases are high which impacts the cost of production and profitability. Sometimes, such dependence on outside suppliers leads to interruptions in supply of raw materials also. These affect the smooth production of the fishnet units.

In view of these problems, more yarn making units shall be started in Kanyakumari district which may eliminate the interruption in supply and variation in raw material prices. A co-operative yarn making unit may be started by the owners of fishnet manufacturing units in Kanyakumari district. The co-operative department of the government of Tamil Nadu may take initiative in this regard.

DEFICIENCY OF FINANCE

Fishnet industry is a capital intensive industry. It needs huge amount of capital both for fixed investments and running expenditure. Therefore, no entrepreneur is able to depend or his/her own source of finance. Most of the fishnet units depend upon external sources to meet their financial requirements. Borrowing from the external sources is a costly one. This leads to a heavy fixed commitment in the form of interest. Even for meeting the regular running expenditure, many fishnet units borrow money from outside sources. The prevailing interest rate in the external market is very high. A portion of the earnings of the fishnet units goes towards meeting the interest obligation. So, the profit of the fishnet units are considerably reduced exclusively because of fixed obligation towards long term and short term loan from external sources of finance.

In order to overcome the above difficulty, the fishnet units, especially the small scale units, must be supplied with adequate financial assistance at a cheaper rate of interest by the banks and the TIIC. The Government should revive the 15 per cent capital subsidy scheme on purchase of machineries. This will reduce the fixed capital burden of the fishnet units. Further, banks and financial institutions may liberally provide loans and advances to fishnet units. Loans may be granted against the mortgage of raw materials and finished goods. Similarly, for working capital requirement cash credit may be liberally sanctioned to fishnet units.

FUNCTIONAL DEFICIENCIES OF FISHNET MANUFACTURES ASSOCIATION

The Fishnet Manufacturers Association of the district does not comprise of all entrepreneurs in the industry especially, the entrepreneurs of small scale fishnet units. The association is dominated by entrepreneurs of big units. Thus, the functioning of Fishnet Manufacturers Association is dominated by the entrepreneurs of big fishnet units. Fishnet Manufacturers Association does not regulate production. Similarly, in no other activity such as marketing of the products, fixing up of the prices, settlement of industrial problems, quality control and maintenance, career guidance and counseling and supply of market information, the association takes part. Strictly speaking, it is inactive and not contributing much towards the growth of fishnet industry in the district. There is no sense of industrial commonness among the entrepreneurs of the fishnet units.

Therefore, a sense of commonness should be developed among the entrepreneurs and all fishnet units should be made the members of the association. The association should be activated with the real spirit of co-operation. The association should be a key role player in the above areas which will strengthen the bargaining power and business prosperity of the entrepreneurs of the fishnet units.

DIFFUSION IN PRODUCTION

It is the production process that determines the cost of a product, quantity of production and its quality. The machinery used for production of fishnet are both domestic made and imported. Most of the fishnet units in the study area have Indian made machines only. The quality and capacity of production vary between Indian made machines and foreign made machines. Generally, Indian made machines are inferior in both the aspects when compared to foreign machineries. This affects the quality of fishnet produced in one side and the cost of fishnet production in another side. Another difficulty in the production process is the lack of technical services in the times of machine breakdowns. In earlier days, the technical services by the makers of the machines were locally available through company's own trained technicians. But now, it is not so. The fishnet unit owners have to depend on their own technicians who are not formally trained but trained through work experience. When the breakdowns are not manageable by the internal technicians, they have to be brought the technicians bring from other fishnet units. These create delays in repair and thus interrupt the production process in one side and increase the cost in another side. Another major problem associated with production is over production of fishnet. As many units are running on three shifts basis and non-stop basis, fishnets are produced irrespective of the demand in the market. This leads to the compulsion for selling at lower prices which ultimately leads to reduction in profit or incurrence of loss.

In view of these problems, the researcher suggests that the quality of indigenous machines must be made on par with that of the foreign makes. The machine manufacturing companies should provide adequate and timely technical services by appointing a permanent team of technicians on regional basis and should give formal training to the technicians of the fishnet companies in repairs and maintenance. In order to avoid over production, the production must be properly matched with the demand in the market and effective programme for increasing market coverage and exploring foreign market should be planned and implemented. Production should be scheduled on the basis of seasonal of demand and all units must declare a weekly holiday which may reduce the production quantity.

INEFFICIENCY IN MARKETING

Ultimately, the success of any business enterprise depends upon its marketing efficiency. The entrepreneurs will be successful only if he/she has the marketing skills and knowledge or he/she is supported by marketing experts. In the fishnet units in Kanyakumari district, in most of the cases, the marketing job is done by the owners themselves. But the owners do not have any formal-education and training in the field of marketing. The language skill needed for marketing their products effectively. Most of the fishnets produced in Kanyakumari district are marketed in the North Indian market which needs proficiency in English and Hindi. But, most of the fishnet unit owners are lacking this skill. Further, the fishnet manufacturers do not adopt any direct marketing strategy. Instead, they rely completely on the wholesale buyers only. Moreover, they are unable to identify the prospects or to avail marketing information with regard to fishnet. All these reduce the marketing efficiency of the fishnet units. Therefore, a special attention is needed is the marketing side of these units. The entrepreneurs should be oriented in the field of marketing and they must be supported with marketing experts as sales managers or sales executives. They should attempt for direct marketing of fishnets to the ultimate consumers that is the fishermen. The Government and the Fishnet Manufacturers Associations should make a good system of marketing information and the entrepreneurs should be supplied with adequate and timely market information.

CONCLUSION

The researcher feels that the study has served the purposes for which it is carried out. As the study is novel one, an attempt has been made by the researcher to explore the avenues as to fulfill the objectives of the study.

Sincere efforts have been made by the researcher to study the growth of fishnet units in Kanyakumari district. Despite the inherent and inevitable limitations of the study, all the specified objectives have been generally arrived at. The researcher hopes that the findings of the study would be of great help for promotion of the fishnet industry. The researcher strongly believes that if the suggestions that are offered in the study are duly considered and if necessary actions are taken by the entrepreneurs of fishnet units in Kanyakumari district, the success and growth are no longer away for fishnet units in Kanyakumari district.

Areas for Future Research

The study is not an end in itself and it will give enough impetus for undertaking further research in the area of fishnet industry in the years to come. In the light of the experience gained through the present study, it has been felt worthwhile to identify some topics for future research. Accordingly, the following topics have been identified and it is left to the future researchers to evaluate the feasibility of undertaking research on these topics:

1. The cost sheet of popular varieties of fishnets manufactured by the fishnet industry in Kanyakumari district;
2. A study on socio-economic welfare of women workers in fishnet units in Kanyakumari district;
3. A study of welfare measures undertaken in the fishnet industry;
4. An impact study of localisation of fishnet industry in Kanyakumari district;
5. The history of fishnet industry in Kanyakumari district — An entrepreneurial approach.

The researcher will feel satisfied if the fishnet units in Kanyakumari district consider the findings useful for decision making in future.

Bibliography

BOOKS

Anderson, Thesis and Assignment writing. New Delhi, Wiley Eastern Limited, 1986.

Anon, Modern Fishing Gear of the World 2. Fishing News (Books) Ltd. London, 1964.

Anon, Modern Fishing Gear of the World. Ed. H. Kristjonsson. Fishing News (Books) Ltd. London, 1959.

Anon, Report of the 1962 Iceland Trawl Mesh Selection Working Group. ICES, 1965, Rep. No. 3.

Anon, The Selectivity of Fishing Gear. Being Volume 2 of the Proceedings of Joint ICNAF/ICES/FAO Special Scientific Meeting, Lisbon 1957. ICNAF Spec., 1963, Pub No. 5.

Aorzano, R., Man-Made Fibres, Bobingen Mills, Germany, 1957.

Ben-yami, A., Study of the Mediterranean Trawl Net. Modern Fishing Gear of the World. H. Kristjohnson [ed.]. Fishing News (Books) Ltd, London, 1959.

Blaxter, J.H.S., Parrish, B.B. and Dickson, W., The Importance of Vision in Fish in Relation to Drifnets and Trawls. Modern Fishing Gear of the World, (ed.) H. Kristjohnson. Fishing News (Books) Ltd, London, 1964, Vol. 2.

Boer, P.A., Trawl Gear Measurements Obtained by Underwater Instruments. ICES North Sea Sub-Committee, 1954, Vol. 4.

Boerema, L.K., Note on the Need for Standardisation of Mesh Measuring Methods. ICES Comparative Fishing Committee, 1958.

Brandt, Fish Catching Methods of the World Revised and Enlarged", Fishing News Books Ltd., London, 1972.

Carrothers, P.T.G., The Physical Properties of Netting and Twines Suitable for Use in Commercial Fishing Gear, Fisheries Research Board of Canada, 1957.

Daniel, R.R., Citizens Report on the State of Development and Environment in Kanyakumari District, South Vision, Chennai, 2001.

Dickson, W. Size Relatively of Trawl Gear in Arctic Surveys. Coun. Meet. int Coun. Explor. Sea., 1988.

Fency Health Reena, S.A. A Descriptive Study of Fishnet Industry in Kanyakumari District, M.Phil. Thesis Unpublished, 2001.

Ferro RST and FG O'Neil, An Overview of Methods of Measuring Twine and Netting Characteristics and Mesh Size ICES CM 1994/B36, 1994.

Ferro, R.S.T. Report by the Study Group on Twin Thickness Measurement. ICES CM, 1983.

Fonteyne, R., U. Link, Stewart, P. and Ward, N., Evaluation of Mesh Measurement Methodologies for Fisheries Inspection and Research. Final Report of the EU Concerted Action FAIR CT96, 1942, 1998.

Galbraith, R.D., Full-scale Instrumented Gear Trials on the ICES Young Fish Sampling Trawl (CHALUT GOV 26/47). Coun. Meet. int. Coun. Explor. Sea, 1986.

Galbraith, R.D., Performance Trails on Chalut 36/47 GOV Constructed in Both Nylon and Polyethylene Twine. Coun. Meet. int. Count. Explor. Sea., 1982.

Gerhard Kulust, Netting Materials for Fishing Gear, London, 1982.

Gopala Krishnan, M., Gazetter of India, Tamil Nadu State, Kanyakumari District, Chennai, 1995.

Grewal, P.S., Methods of Statistical Analysis, Sterling Publishers Pvt. Ltd., New Delhi, 1990.

Gupta, S.P., Statistical Methods, Sultan Chand and Sons, New Delhi, 1985.

Hayhurst, G.A. and Robinson, A., Construction and Numbering of Synthetic Net Twines, William Kenyen and Sons Ltd., U.K., 1959.

Horn, W., Rationalization of Sole Fisheries of Means of Electrified Beam Trawls. In: Report of the Working Group on Research on Engineering Aspects of Fishing Gear, Vessels and Equipment, ICES, 1976.

Isaken, B. and Valdmarsen, J.W., Selectivity Experiments with Square Mesh Contends in Bottom Trawls. Coun. Meet. int. Count. Explor. Sea., 1986.

Isaken, B.Lisovsky, S., Larsen, R.B. and Sakhnoe, V., Results from the Joint Russian-Norwegian Selectivity Experiments on Cod (Gadus morhua L.) in the Barents Sea with 55 mm Sorting Grid Systems. In Report of the Study Group on Grid (Grate) Sorting Systems in Trawls, Beam Trawls and Seine Nets. Vol. 1, 1995.

Klust, G., Netting Materials for Fishing Gear. Fishing News (Book) Ltd, Oxford, 1973.

Klust, Gerhad, Efficiency of Synthetic Fibres in Fishing, Institute for Nets and Twines Ltd., Hamburg, 1967.

Kristjohnson Hilmar, Modern Fishing Gear of the World, Food and Agricultural Organisation (FAO), London, 1957.

Lonsdals, J.E., Nylon in Fishing Nets, British Nylon Spinners Ltd, Lyods, 1992.

Lusyne, P.A., Some Consideration in Net Marketing, Food and Agricultural Organisation (FAO), Fisheries Division, Frankfurt, 1987.

MacLennan, D.N., Evaluation of Gear Performance by Physical Measurement; State of the Art and a Forward Look. ICES C.M, 1970.

Ministry of Commerce and Industry, Nylon Fishing Nets, Government of India, New Delhi, 1960.

Nair Rajan, N., Marketing, Sultan Chand and Sons, New Delhi, 1994.

Reuter, J., Rusting of Materials Used in Fishing, Tital Publication, Hongkong, 1997.

Shimozaki, Yoshinori, Characteristics of Synthetic Twines Used for Fishing Nets and Ropes in Japan, Tokai Regional Fisheries Research Technology, Japan, 1987.

Singh, Jai, P., Fishes of Kanyakumari, Sharon Press, Karinkal, Kanyakumari District, 1976.

Sinha, R.K., Marine Resources and Applicable Laws, Common Wealth Publishers, New Delhi, 1996.

Stewart, P.A.M., Measurement of the Headline Heights of Gill Nets in Tidal Flows. Coun. Meet. int. Coun. Explor. Sea. C.M. 1986, 1976.

Stutz, Hans, Terminology and Count of Synthetic Fibre Twines for Fishing Purpose, Bobingen Mills, Germany, 1995.

Tauti, M., A Relation Between Experiments on Model and Full Scale of Fishing Nets. Bulletin of Japanese Society of Scientific Fisheries, 1934, Vol. 4.

Von Brandt, A., Standardisation and Fishing Gear. ICES, 1969

Walsh, S.J., The 1997 Theme Session on the Catching Performance of Fishing Gears used in Surveys ICES J. mar. Sci., 1999, No. 56.

Wardle, C.S., Fish Reaction to Fishing Gears. Scottish Fisheries Bullettin, 1976, No. 43.

Westhoff, C.J.W. Description of the Latest Version of a Longitudinal Spring-loaded Mesh Measuring Gauge with Automatic Stop. Paper Presented to the ICES Comparative Fishing Committee.

Westhoff, C.J.W., Pope, J.W. and Beverton, R.J.H., The ICES Mesh Gauge. Charlottenlund Slot, 1962.

Wijagaarden, Van, J.K., Testing Methods for Net Twines and Nets, Research Laboratory, Netherland, 1986.

Wileman, D.A., Ferro, R.S.T., Fonteyne, R. and Millar, R.B., Manual of Methods of Measuring the Selectivity of Towed Fishing Gears. ICES Co-operative Research Report 215, 1996.

Wileman, D.A., Flume Tank Facility — Net Modelling Techniques. ICES, 1976.

Wright Sidney, Curious Methods of Fishing in the World Marvels of the World Fisheries, Logos Press, New Delhi, 1986.

Zaucha, J., Evaluation of Rot-Retarding Net Preservatives, Sea Fisheries Institute, Poland, 1998.

REPORTS

A Census of Tamil Nadu Marine Fishermen, Directorate of Fisheries, Government of Tamil Nadu, Madras, 1986.

A Statistical Hand Book of Tamil Nadu, Government of Tamil Nadu, Department of Statistics, Madras.

Development of Small Scale Fisheries Improvement of Large-Mesh Different for small-Scale Fisheries in Sri Lanka, 1980.

Integrated Fisheries Project, Cochin, October 1997.

Small Industry Scheme No. 59, Nylon Fishing Nets, Development Commissioner (Small Scale Industry), Ministry of Commerce and Industry. Government of India, New Delhi.

Statistical Abstract of Kanyakumari District, Department of Statistics, Government of Tamil Nadu, Madras, 1977-1993.

Tamil Nadu Fisheries at a Glance, Nagercoil, 2000.

Tamil Nadu Marine Fisherfolk Census Director of Fisheries, Chennai, 2000.

The Study Conducted on the Organisational Structure and Functioning of Kerala Fisheries Corporation Nylon Net Factory, Ernakulam, 1992.

The Tamil Nadu Fisheries Manual, Department of Fisheries, Government of Tamil Nadu, Madras, 1971.

Index